YOUR PATHWAY TO A NEW LIFE
AND LASTING FREEDOM

JOURNEY OF
TRANSFORMATION
SCOTT REALL

CREATE THE LIFE YOU'VE ALWAYS WANTED

Cover photo by Cristina Conti/Shutterstock

Cover design by Linda Bourdeaux/thedesigndesk.com

To find a Restore Small Group near you, please visit the following website: www.restoresmallgroups.org.

If you would like to invite Scott to speak to your church, community organization, or event, please visit www.restoresmallgroups.org

If you would like to donate to Restore Small Groups to help support the life-changing work of this ministry, please visit www.restoresmallgroups.org.

ISBN: 979-8-9889747-2-7

TABLE OF CONTENTS

SHAPING OUR LIVES FOR THE DIVINE

Do you ever wish you had a different life? Do you ever think about what it would look like and feel like to have the life you've always wanted? Would you like to start over? Maybe you've been battling an addiction and you long to make a new start. Maybe you've just suffered through a nasty divorce and hit a wall. Maybe your weight has gotten out of control and you've given up on a new you. Maybe you've chosen the wrong career path or experienced a health scare. Now you are ready to create the life you've always wanted. But you may not know how to break the habit of being yourself.

A few years ago, I longed for a new start. I was struggling with loneliness and despair. Everything in my life had become so complicated, which triggered a litany of toxic emotions that were suffocating me. I wasn't sure where these emotions originated. But I was being consumed with thoughts of fear, shame, insecurity, and doubt. And I couldn't understand why. So, I started peeling back the layers of my past narrative. I went all the way back to my childhood. I asked myself, "Where did all of this fear, shame, insecurity, and doubt originate?"

As a young boy, I suffered from night terrors, where a dark figure would pin me down and suffocate me. I would wake the whole house with my screaming and thrashing around trying to free myself. It would take some shaking to wake me and get me out of the night terror. Once fully awake, I felt broken—like something was wrong with me at the core of my being. All the while my bewildered parents looked on helplessly.

I felt humiliated for being terrified and out of control.

Now fast-forward to the age of fifteen. I was in a bad car accident. The car flipped over and landed on top of me. It crushed my face into the pavement—ripping off my nose and blowing up my right eye. What was so terrifying was that it was dark outside and I was fully conscious. I was drowning in a pool of my own blood. I tried hard to free myself but couldn't. I was trapped. I couldn't get out. It was very reminiscent of the night terrors I had as a little boy. Once again, I was being trapped and suffocated by a dark figure, but this time it was a car. I remember being trapped under that car, fully awake, and fully aware that I was dying . . . just like the night terrors. I also felt such a sense of shame about the choice I had made to get in the car that night. I felt my actions would hurt my parents deeply.

The ambulance arrived and concerned faces rushed me to the hospital. Hours later in the recovery room, nurses told me not to touch my face. I knew it was bad when they refused to let me look in a mirror.

For years after the car wreck, every car ride terrified me. My mind would not calm down. I felt vulnerable and out of control. Even though my face and injuries had healed, no one talked to me about the mental trauma. I was left to figure it out on my own. I kept feeling trapped beneath the wreckage. Suffocating in my own blood. This feeling would hit me out of nowhere and I'd be right back in the trauma. It shook me to the core with fear. I no longer saw the world as a place of possibilities. The world became a place where things die and I developed a fear of death that followed me into adulthood. The memory of the car wreck became my nightmare and I developed a deep-rooted paradigm of fear, insecurity, shame, and doubt from which I viewed the world, God, and myself.

Now fast-forward to early adulthood. This fear-based/shame-based paradigm controlled my life choices and kept me in psychological pain. Soon I turned to a series of addictions and attachments to numb myself, only making things worse. To stabilize my crisis, I entered a twelve-step program, where I treated the symptoms of the addictions but did not change my fear-based mindset.

Twenty-five years later—when I realized this—my present struggle became clear. My deep-rooted paradigm of fear, insecurity, shame, and doubt controlled my life, and the root of fear reached back to my childhood. It had never been dealt with completely. I'd never broken the habit of being that terrified child. Whenever I faced adversity, this fear created the same thoughts that created the same choices, the same actions, the same experiences, and the same feelings that originated in this past experience. I was living in an emotional hell.

Around the time I made this discovery, I read something from Stephen Covey that he calls "hacking at the leaves." The practice of "hacking at the leaves" is dealing with the symptoms of our problems, instead of striking at the root. He writes, "We can only achieve quantum improvements in our lives as we quit hacking at the leaves of attitude and behavior and get to work on the root, the paradigms from which our attitudes and behaviors flow."[1] Understanding how a past experience controlled my emotions and created my mindset was a game changer for my transformation. I knew I had to strike at the root of the problem from which my attitudes and behaviors flowed. I agree with Dr. Joe Dispenza,

> "Here is how it works: You have an experience, which has an emotional charge. Then you have a thought about the particular past event. The thought becomes a memory, which then reflexively reproduces the emotion of the experience. If you keep thinking about that memory repeatedly, the thought, the memory, and the emotion merge as one, and you 'memorize' the emotion . . . for true change to occur, it is essential to "unmemorize" an emotion that has become part of your personality."[2]

Creating the life we've always wanted means striking at the root of the false self we've fashioned from past experiences. We "unmemorize" toxic emotions and live from an authentic vision of our inner life. To do this, we will start with identity and not with conduct. We will start in the realm of the mind, not in behavior modification. We must not think of ourselves as the person who does this or that wrong thing. Instead, we must realize our identity as a beloved child of God.

Our study will focus on two Bible passages that show how to create this new life. The main Scripture I will be returning to throughout our study together is found in Romans 12:2:

> "Do not conform to the pattern of this world, but be transformed by the renewing of your mind. Then you will be able to test and approve what God's will is—his good, pleasing and perfect will."

The other one comes from Ephesians 4:22-24:

> "You were taught, with regard to your former way of life, to put off your old self, which is being corrupted by its deceitful desires; to be made new in the attitude of your minds; and to put on the new self, created to be like God in true righteousness and holiness."

Familiarize yourself with these two passages. We will be returning to them throughout our time together. You may want to write them down on a note card or in a journal and meditate on them each day.

The two words from these scriptures I will focus on are: *conform* and *transform*. When we conform, we assume an outward expression and our behavior is adapted from the outer world around us. We have conformed our behavior to the patterns of this world. Then we are like actors masquerading as something we are not. We are putting on a false self that is not an expression of our true self. But when we put on the new self, the attitude of our mind changes and we transform. "Therefore, if anyone is in Christ, the new creation has come: The old has gone, the new is here (2 Corinthians 5:17). We do everything to make our outward world match our inner being. We live from a place of authenticity. We are new beings.

D. Martyn Lloyd-Jones says we should think of it like a Christmas tree at Christmastime. Back in the day, people would hang artificial fruit on their trees—silver and gold apples and pears (I'm sure this practice continues). The artificial is that which is put on the tree. When you go into an orchard you see apples and pears, but they are real. They have grown from the inner life of the tree—this is at the heart of transformation.[3] We empty out the artificial junk and replace it with an inner life rooted in the life of Christ, the true vine, which allows us to grow the fruit of the spirit—love, joy, peace, forbearance, kindness, goodness, faithfulness, gentleness and self-control (Galatians 5:22-23). This is how we cocreate with God a new way to see ourselves and the world. Everything else is just artificial fruit. It's just hacking at the leaves. In this study, we will focus on renewing our minds, not our behavior, because what needs to change is what controls the mind. We need to take control of the direction of our thoughts for them to be changed. Our inward state accomplishes this.

OUR MINDSET

We see life through our own unique lens. This is our mindset. It's everything we think about ourselves and the world around us. It's our internal model. Changing our mindset is the great key principle to spirituality. It all starts with renewing our mind. The interior processes of the mind—which direct our thoughts—must be renewed, not the mind itself. We must train our minds to think differently because we are new creations. We have a new identity. James Clear writes, "It's hard to change your habits if you never change the underlying beliefs that led to your past behavior. You have a new goal and a new plan, but you haven't changed who you are."[4] He goes on to say that if we never shift the way we look at ourselves, then the old identity can sabotage our new plans for change. I agree! What will make the difference is the kind of identity we create.

In our time together, we will think of identity as a self-defining story. Dan P. McAdams calls it "the psychology of life stories."[5] He suggests that identity itself takes the form of story, complete with setting, scenes, character, plot, and theme. He believes that we reconstruct the personal past, perceive the present, and anticipate the future in terms of an internalized and evolving self-story. It's the idea that identity is an internalized life story that is growing and transforming.

Life stories are based on biographical facts, but they go considerably beyond the facts. They are psychosocial constructions, coauthored by us and our cultural context that give our lives meaning. And this transformation—as you will see—takes place inside the psychology of our life story. It creates a mindset from which we interact with the world around us. I call this interaction the plotline of our story. It's our personal paradigm. When we remember the experiences of our lives, we remember our experience in story form. Memories are images in the brain that become edited video clips that are arranged into cinema-like structures and stored for retrieval. Not everything gets remembered, only the highlights, which can create problems. I will be walking us through piecing together our life stories to better understand why we are making certain decisions and responding to adversity in less-than-optimal ways.

Inside your evolving self-story, you will discover your true identity and true meaning. I'll show you how positive and negative elements can synergize and create a redemption story. We are all different. Life stories abound with complexity and variety, and I am not looking to make you into someone you're not or into a clone of someone else. Your dynamic and evolving narrative constitutes your individuality, situated in a particular family and among friends and acquaintances.[6]

Self-understanding starts with the past and leads to a new identity. This is our goal. So in the pages that follow, I'll show you how to construct and cocreate with God a new identity and a new paradigm to live from. Then out of this vision we will create a step-by-step plan on how to create the life you've always wanted. Because negative thoughts are the result of some past experience that has an emotion embedded in the experience, we will go deeper than just telling you to "think positive thoughts." Our fear-based/shame-based paradigms have an origin story that produce the negativity. We never change our thoughts without "unmemorizing" the emotion embedded in the past experience that created the backstory of our lives. For the next six weeks, I will teach you how habits form and how paradigms work in the mind, and then the principals on how to rewire your brain and create the life you've always wanted. By learning these things, you will discover God's good, pleasing, and perfect will.

For six weeks, we will explore how the mind can be renewed and how this renewal transforms our past narratives. In the first two weeks, we will establish some basic rules about habit formation and paradigm shifts. We will discuss overarching themes and principles that we will return to throughout our time together.

In the third and fourth weeks, we will investigate our thought processes.

In week five, I'll teach you how to detach from your past selves and how to make a new start. We will rewrite the endings to our stories using a coherent narrative about how you got from the past to the present. Then we will lay down richer memories.

In week six, we will shape our brains to participate with the Divine. We will learn how to cocreate with God the life we've always wanted.

Each chapter will have practices at the end to help you further understand your paradigm and how to change it. At the completion of our study, you will have emptied out your toxic paradigm and created a new mindset of hope, health, and happiness. Let's put your old life behind you and create the life you've always wanted!

FIXED MINDSET VS. GROWTH MINDSET

THE MINDSET OF POSSIBILITY

Where there is no vision, the people perish . . .
—PROVERBS 29:18

A bride accompanied her fiancé to the Hyatt Hotel in downtown Boston in 1990 to plan what was supposed to be their wedding banquet. They poured over the menu, made selections of fine china and silver, pointed to the pictures of flower arrangements they liked—the bill came to $13,000, which was an expensive sum back in 1990. After leaving a check for half that amount as a down payment, the couple went home to flip through books of wedding announcements.

The day the announcements were supposed to hit the mailbox, the potential groom got cold feet. "I'm just not sure," he said, "it's a big commitment. Let's think about this a little bit longer." In the end, he dumped his fiancée.

When the jilted bride returned to the Hyatt to cancel the banquet, the Events Manager could not have been more understanding. "The same thing happened to me, honey," she said and told the story of her own broken engagement. But about the refund, she had bad news. "The contract is binding. You're only entitled to $1,300 back. You have two options, forfeit the rest of the down payment (thousands of dollars) or go ahead with the banquet. I'm sorry—really, I am."

It seemed crazy, but the more the jilted bride thought about it, the more she liked the idea of going ahead with the party. Not a wedding banquet, mind you, but a big blow-out. Ten years before, the jilted bride had been living in a homeless shelter. She'd gotten back on her feet, found a good job, set aside a sizable nest egg. Now she had this wild notion of using her savings to treat the down and outs of Boston to a night on the town. And so it was in June of 1990 the Hyatt Hotel in downtown Boston hosted a party such as it had never seen before. The hostess changed the menu to boneless chicken in honor of the groom, she said. She sent invitations to rescue missions and homeless shelters, and on that warm summer night, people who were used to dumpster diving for food dined instead on chicken cordon bleu. Hyatt waiters in tuxedos served hors d'oeuvres to senior citizens propped up by crutches and aluminum walkers. Bag ladies, vagrants, and addicts took one night off from the hard life on the sidewalks outside and instead sipped champagne and ate chocolate wedding cake and danced to Big Band melodies late into the night.[7]

Don't you admire her? She didn't allow herself to be a victim of rejection. She transformed her moment of shame by looking at it differently. She didn't avoid the pain of it. She took a bad situation and put a new spin on it. If she would have chosen to look at her circumstances through the toxic thought, "I'm not worthy of love," what kind of future would have been possible for her? Plus, it would have changed her core identity. She would have changed the way she valued herself and the way she perceived the world. "I'm a victim." Then this paradigm would have spawned even more toxic thoughts.

HAVING A PARADIGM SHIFT

To change a toxic core paradigm and create a new mindset, we need a *paradigm shift*. Stephen Covey defines a paradigm shift he once experienced like this: "Suddenly I *saw* things differently, and because I *saw* things differently, I *thought* differently, I *felt* differently, I *behaved* differently."[8] A paradigm shift is a fundamental shift in thinking. (I will use the word paradigm and mindset interchangeably throughout this book.) "Paradigms are powerful because they create the lens through which we see the world."[9] This is mindset.

PARADIGM SHIFT

A fundamental change in approach or underlying assumptions; An important change that happens when the usual way of thinking about or doing something is replaced by a new and different way.

The jilted bride had a paradigm shift. She was able to see rejection differently, which originated from a core paradigm of love and security. She basically said, "Okay, let's look at this differently. What can I do to see this through a lens of love and acceptance?" Her paradigm shift created a new ending to her failed wedding plans. She didn't allow the fiancé to ruin her life when he backed out. She rescripted it and created something new out of it.

Viktor Frankl says, "Between stimulus and response there is a space. In that space is our power to choose our response. In our response lies our growth and our freedom."[10] The jilted bride suffered the stimulus of a broken engagement and was able to choose her response. The new attitude of her mind created new growth and freedom. This is the fundamental law of growth. We must be free to choose our response, or we make ourselves the victim and stunt our growth. We never change a self-defeating, fixed mindset until we experience a paradigm shift. The way we see the world must shift. *Possibility* must become a new *actuality*. We believe in the possibility of change, which creates the actuality of change. **Until we establish a core paradigm of love and acceptance, we will never think differently or see the world differently.** Our old mindset of feeling unworthy of love makes us think the same thoughts that create the same choices, the same actions, the same experiences, and the same feelings, which originates from our fixed mindset of failure.[11]

Dr. Joe Dispenza writes, "So if we want to change some aspect of our reality, we have to think, feel, and act in new ways; we have to 'be' different in terms of our responses to experiences. We have to 'become' someone else. We have to create a new state of mind . . . we need to observe a new outcome with that new mind."[12]

We are responsible for the thoughts we think and how these thoughts make us behave. It's a function of our decisions, not our conditions. And the way we choose to see things is a choice. The jilted bride made a choice to see things differently and rewrote the ending to her story.

Sometimes we spend too much time asking, "Why?" And we never get around to asking, "Now what? What's next? What do I want my final outcome to look like? How can I write the ending to my story?" Brené Brown writes, "When we have the courage to walk into our story and own it, we get to write the ending. And when we don't own our stories of failure, setbacks, and hurt—they own us."[13] This was the thought process of the jilted bride. I think she knew her hurt would own her, so she refused to be the victim. She responded with a mindset of possibility.

CHOOSE YOUR MINDSET AND CHOOSE YOUR OUTCOME

We see life through our own unique lens. This is our mindset. It's what we believe about ourselves and the world around us. Carol Dweck says we have either a *fixed mindset* or a *growth mindset*.

In the fixed mindset, we believe our qualities are carved in stone. Success is about proving we're smart or talented. Validating ourselves. We believe failure is having a setback. Getting a bad grade. Losing a tournament. Getting fired. Getting rejected. It means we're not smart or talented enough for success. And there's nothing we can do to change that.

FIXED MINDSET
Belief that you are either good or bad at something based on your inherent nature

GROWTH MINDSET
Belief that your most basic abilities can be developed through dedication and hard work

In the growth mindset, we believe our basic qualities are things we can cultivate through our efforts, our strategies, and help from others. We become new beings with a new attitude. We are ready to grow and develop ourselves. Effort is what makes us smart or talented. It has nothing to do with failure. We cannot fail if we are training. Trying to do something means failure is possible. Growth is training toward a goal.

Mindsets are just beliefs. They're powerful beliefs, but they're just something in your mind, and you can change your mind.[14]

Having the growth mindset is what I'm advocating in this book. Transformation is possible when we enter the growth mindset. If we have a fixed mindset, then we will use temporary fixes and attachments to relieve the pain of failure, which compounds our problems, then nothing productive is ultimately going to happen. We will give in and give up. St. Gregory of Nyssa said in the fourth century, "Sin happens whenever we refuse to keep growing."[15] This, in a sense, was my problem—the fixed mindset of fear kept me from growing through the years.

Cocreating a growth mindset with God—a new way of seeing our world—is how God's character takes root in us. We see beyond our old reality and beyond our old narratives of past failure. We will get into this more throughout our study together. But it all begins with what we are willing to see and how we interpret what we see. Fear, shame, insecurity, and doubt can distort perception and create hopelessness about the future. Don't allow the shame of the past to predict the future.

We have a choice about what we are willing to see and do.

Do you have a fixed mindset? Then change will be difficult if not impossible. I'm not asking you to be perfect or change a bad habit or believe in some form of fake positive affirmation right from the start. But you must be willing to make a paradigm shift and move into a growth mindset. "When people believe their basic qualities can be developed, failures may still hurt, but failures don't define them. And if abilities can be expanded—if change and growth are possible—then there are still many paths to success."[16] The jilted bride had a growth mindset and believed another ending to her failed wedding plans existed.

The life you've always wanted is available if we can see it, believe it, and push through our failure to the other side. This is the journey to transformation. Another ending to life is possible. We just need to take a different point of view than the one that led us to despair. I had to believe my life wasn't over after the car wreck—that I could make a new start.

This is what I'm asking: "Can you make a new start?" How you answer this question is fundamental to having a growth mindset. Answering yes means a new ending to your story awaits you.

REFLECTIONS

1. How would you respond to being dumped like the jilted bride?

2. Do you believe you have a growth mindset or a fixed mindset?

THE MESSAGE OF THE SNARE

*Surely he will save you from the fowler's snare
and from the deadly pestilence. He will cover you with
his feathers, and under his wings you will find refuge;
his faithfulness will be your shield and rampart.*

—PSALM 91:3—4

A bazaar was held in a village in northern India. Everyone brought their wares to trade and sell. One old farmer brought in a whole covey of quail. He had tied a string around one leg of each bird. The other ends of all the strings were tied to a ring which fit loosely over a central stick. He had taught the quail to walk dolefully in a circle, around and around, like a carousel. Nobody seemed interested in buying the birds until a devout Brahman came along. He believed in the Hindu idea of respect for all life, so his heart of compassion went out to those poor little creatures walking in their monotonous circles.

"I want to buy them all," he told the merchant, who was elated. After receiving the money, he was surprised to hear the buyer say, "Now, I want you to set them all free."

"What's that, sir?"

"You heard me. Cut the strings from their legs and turn them loose. Set them all free!"

With a shrug, the old farmer bent down and snipped the strings off the quail. They were free at last. What happened? The birds simply continued marching around and around in a circle. Finally, the man had to shoo them away. But they landed some distance away and resumed their predictable march. Free, unfettered, released . . . yet they kept going around in circles as if still tied.[17]

Why couldn't these birds see, feel, or understand their freedom? No doubt they had tried to free themselves early on, but eventually they believed the message of the snare: "You're trapped." Now it was part of their automatic system. They were caught in a fixed mindset.

Maybe, you also have stopped believing you can be free. Whether you realize it or not, you are bound by a message of the snare. Like the birds, we can conform to the pattern of this world (earthbound circles) and need our minds renewed to escape. Romans 12:2 says, "Do not conform to the pattern of this world, but be transformed by the renewing of your mind." We never make a new start with a mind entrenched in a toxic paradigm of fear, shame, insecurity, and doubt. Remember that mindsets are just powerful beliefs.

Dr. Joe Dispenza writes,

> "A belief is just an extended state of being—essentially, beliefs are thoughts and feelings (attitudes) that you keep thinking and feeling over and over again until you hardwire them in your brain and emotionally condition them into your body. You could say you become addicted to them, which is why it's so hard to change them and why it doesn't feel good on a gut level when they're challenged. Because experiences are neurologically etched into your brain (causing you to think), and chemically embodied as emotions (causing you to feel), your beliefs are based on past memories."[18]

So when you visit the same thoughts over and over by thinking about and analyzing what you remember from your past, these thoughts will fire and wire into an automatic unconscious program. This automatic, unconscious paradigm must be challenged at the root. Let's say your toxic belief is: "I'm unworthy of God's love."

Transforming this message begins with understanding the unconditional love of God. We all have this desire to be loved by God. It's the deepest longing in our soul—to love God and be loved by Him. Gerald May believes this desire gives us meaning. He writes, "Regardless of how we describe it, it is longing for love. It is a hunger to love, to be loved, and to move closer to the Source of love. This yearning is the essence of the human spirit; it is the origin of our highest hopes and most noble dreams."[19]

Why do we stop pursuing the Source of love? Sometimes it's because we don't see ourselves as worthy of this love. Unless we see ourselves as beloved children of God, we will never transform. We form the belief that this kind of love is not attainable for us any longer because we are broken, shameful, and unworthy of love. Then we settle on conditional love and believe, "Why would God want to love me? Look at what I've done to the mistakes I've made. I'm unlovable." But is this true? Asking this question will send you on a quest to understand why you don't feel loved by God. Where is this thought coming from? What has happened to make you feel unlovable and rejected by God?

Rob Bell writes,

> "The issue then isn't my beating myself up over all of the things I am not doing or the things I am doing poorly; the issue is my learning who this person is, who God keeps insisting I already am . . . God is retelling each of our stories in Jesus. All of the bad parts and the ugly parts and the parts we want to pretend never happened are redeemed. Our choice becomes this: We can trust his retelling of the story, or we can trust our telling of our story. It is a choice we make every day about the reality we are going to live in."[20]

Who does God keep insisting you are? We must see what God sees in us. This will be at the heart of our study together. Until I see myself as loved by God, then I will never live free. I will always perpetuate the belief: "I'm unworthy of love." I'll feel guilty and shameful. But God keeps insisting that we are new creations. "Therefore, if anyone is in Christ, the new creation has come: The old has gone, the new is here" (2 Corinthians 5:17). But we say, "I'm not new. I'm the same old sinner." We have a hard time letting ourselves be loved by God because our self-defeating thoughts and behaviors keep sabotaging our efforts. Much like the message of the snare that kept the birds grounded, we don't fly even though we are free.

We will never offer love or receive love as long as we believe we are unworthy of love. Why would we attract love if this is our state of being? Until we love ourselves, we are not open to love. We can't love our neighbor as ourselves (Matthew 22:39) because we don't love ourselves. And to take it a step further: We can't love God with all our heart and with all our soul and with all our mind (Matthew 22:37), if we think He doesn't love us. We will always be one step removed from the possibility of His love and living by the rules of conditional love if we say "God will only love me if I _____ (fill in the blank)."

The prodigal son, in Jesus's "Parable of the Lost Son," left home and squandered his inheritance. When he thought about returning home, he wrote a speech to give his father upon his return: "Father, I have sinned against heaven and against you. I am no longer worthy to be called your son. Make me like one of your hired servants" (Luke 15:11-32). The prodigal son made the mistake of forecasting his future by referencing his past.

But the prodigal's father welcomed him home and put a ring on his finger and a robe on his back. His father never said the prodigal was unworthy to be his son. The prodigal created this toxic belief inside his own mind. He thought he could only be loved conditionally. And the one making this decision was the prodigal son, not the father. We do the same thing with God. We dictate our own terms.

If you are like most people, you have a long column of debt in your accounting system where you have failed. Wouldn't it be great to erase all the guilt and condemnation and see yourself as a new creation? It happened to the prodigal. He experienced a new relationship with his father based on a new self—one that experienced grace. This is my hope for you as we travel this sacred path—that you will experience grace and see yourself as a new creation.

Let Christ love you and awaken within you the possibility for love. Let His intimacy back inside. Isn't that what intimacy is? *In-to-me-see.* See yourself with the eyes and mind of Christ. Then allow yourself to be loved. With a fresh new start, you will be moved to become the person God keeps insisting you are. Disconnect from the past because studies have shown that if you do "faults of a remote, past self are less apt to tarnish (your) present self-image."[21] Seeing yourself as a new person will motivate you to be more in line with the person you want to become.

The devout Brahman kept insisting the birds were free. Who had the wrong message? The birds or the Brahman? God is like the Brahman. He sees you free. But nothing changes if you can't experience a paradigm shift and see it for yourself. So stop allowing your old self to terrorize you. Move into a new relationship with the Source of love. This is the paradigm shift to the new you. See yourself as a person worthy of love. Let yourself be loved. Do this and the chains will fall off and you will learn to fly again. The ultimate paradigm is seeing ourselves through the eyes of unconditional love.

Are you tired of going in circles when you were meant to soar? Are you willing to let yourself be loved?

REFLECTIONS:

1. Do you feel unworthy of love?

2. What is keeping you from feeling worthy?

3. Who does God say you are?

BETWEEN STIMULUS AND RESPONSE

Our behavior is a function of our decisions, not our conditions.

—STEPHEN R. COVEY

A reporter investigating the citrus industry in Florida went into a shed where he saw a man sorting oranges. As the oranges tumbled down the conveyor belt, the man went to work putting large oranges in the large holes, the small oranges in the small holes, and the bruised oranges in another hole.

The reporter watched this man perform his incredibly boring job until he couldn't stand it any longer. Finally, he asked the man, "Doesn't it get to you? I mean, how can you stand putting those oranges into those holes all day long?"

"You don't know the half of it," said the man. "From the time I come in until the time I leave, it's decisions, decisions, decisions!"[22]

Someone once said that every decision is a desire to solve a problem. Do you ever question why you are choosing a certain response to your problems? Or do you just react without much thought? If you have a fixed mindset, you are probably not questioning the validity of your response. You are allowing your emotions to take over, which makes it difficult to make the right decision. Imagine if the man sorting oranges made his decisions by what he felt about each orange, instead of what he observed. His decisions wouldn't match the proof.

Are your decisions matching who you are wishing to become? Think back to our discussion about the prodigal son. He decided to feed pigs, which didn't match who he was as a Jewish boy. It took him further into bondage, because a good Jewish boy would never get involved with swine. It goes against everything that defines him as being Jewish.

We must always hold central the person we wish to become. Having a changeless sense of who you are, what you are about, and what you value is vital. Because what we value determines what we do. You must have a vision of what the authentic, free you will look like. This is how we create the life we've always wanted. We make decisions that lead us in this direction, and these decisions are always made between stimulus and response.

Viktor Frankl wrote, "Between stimulus and response there is a space. In that space is our power to choose our response. In our response lies our growth and our freedom."[23] What we do between the moment a crisis hits and the moment we choose our response is what is meant by "between stimulus and response." In this sacred moment, we can make a decision. But the fixed mindset tells us there is no choice. Our situation is permanent. We are helpless and hopeless, so we give-in to our fixed mindsets, instead of choosing to live free and entering the growth mindset.

People who give up and give in to their circumstances believe they don't have a choice between stimulus and response. Their fixed mindset tells them they can't choose their response because it's too late. They are too broken and don't have what it takes to create a new life.

Aaron Beck tells couples in counseling never to think these fixed-mindset thoughts like, "My partner is incapable of change." or " Nothing can improve our relationship."[24] These thoughts doom every marriage. In Numbers 11, these fixed thoughts haunted the children of Israel's relationship with God. Their response to adversity was a conditioned, hardwired negative response: "We're enslaved. We're trapped. We're going to die." We see this in the children of Israel throughout their time in the wilderness. The children of Israel kept bringing everything back to what they had in Egypt. God would deliver them from adversity, then they would forget and just go back to automatic doubting and complaining. They couldn't overcome the influence of their fixed mindset. God could never seem to purge them of their ideas rooted in slavery. They hated manna from heaven. They wanted to eat like they did in Egypt. Whenever water seemed scarce and the road difficult, they wanted to go back to slavery in Egypt. Their old narratives of Egypt kept influencing their present reality. Nothing improved their relationship with God. They were like the covey of quail the Brahman freed. They kept going in circles in the desert.

Egypt should have been far from their minds, but they kept returning to its old narrative. It was a conditioned response. They were not making decisions between stimulus and response that would create the life they wanted. It takes deliberate practice to break a stronghold of thoughts that are wired together—for the thoughts that fire together, wire together. And it takes self-awareness and paying attention to the space of possibility between stimulus and response.

Sports psychologist Kevin Elko calls it choosing to be the thermometer or the thermostat. He writes:

> "A thermometer, of course, reflects the temperature in the room; it tells you whether it is hot or cold, gives you a reading on what it's like outside or in the building or room where you are. My observation is that most people are like thermometers. They reflect what's going on around them, what the circumstances of their lives are . . . People who are thermostats don't sit and wait for life to happen to them. They cause life to happen. If a situation is not so good, they don't just reflect that; they give energy and hope to the situation, they reveal what might be possible."[25]

What about you? Are you a thermostat or thermometer? Do you allow circumstances to control your thoughts and feelings? When the fixed mindset, such as—I will never change or they will never change—is running your thoughts and actions, you will think the same thoughts that create the same choices, the same actions, the same experiences, and the same feelings. This makes us thermometers.

We always have a choice between stimulus and response to be a thermometer or a thermostat. Stephen Covey writes, "It's not what happens to us, but our response to what happens to us that hurts us. Between stimulus and response is our greatest power—the freedom to choose."[26] Only you can give energy to God's plans for your life. You are in charge of the attitude of your mind (Ephesians 4:22–24).

Are you manufacturing joy or unhappiness? Joyful people are proactive. They give their lives positive energy. "Finally, brothers and sisters, whatever is true, whatever is noble, whatever is right, whatever is pure, whatever is lovely, whatever is admirable—if anything is excellent or praiseworthy—think about such things" (Philippians 4:8). Choosing these life-giving things infuses your life with possibility. It's the choice between stimulus and response that gives energy to your world.

REFLECTIONS:

1. Are you a thermometer or a thermostat?

2. Do you think you can choose a different response to your problems or are they all automatic?

3. What tends to make you give up?

OUR EXPECTATIONS
SHAPE OUR OUTCOMES

Never be afraid to trust an unknown future to a known God.

—CORRIE TEN BOOM

A recent *New York Times* article reported on a study about maids and their work. At the start of the study, Harvard psychologist Ellen Langler asked 84 maids about their daily exercise regiments. Fully a third of the women said they got no exercise at all, while two-thirds said they did not work out on a regular basis. Then Langler and her team took measurements of the women's basic fitness levels, which indicated that they had the poor health of people who are basically sedentary. Then the researchers deceived 44 of the maids by telling them that cleaning 15 rooms daily—pushing recalcitrant vacuum cleaners, scrubbing tubs, pulling sheets—constitutes more than enough activity to meet the surgeon general's recommendation of a half-hour of physical activity daily. The researchers even provided specifics: 15 minutes of scrubbing burns 60 calories, 15 minutes of vacuuming burns 50. They posted the information in the maids' lounges for daily reminders. The other 40 maids in the study were not informed that their work equaled exercise.

A month later the average maid in the first study group had lost 2 pounds, their blood pressure dropped by 10 points—by all measurements the 44 maids were "significantly healthier." The 40 maids in the second control group had no change.

Why did the 44 maids get "significantly healthier?" They had only changed their mindset, not their behavior. The work routine was the same for all 84 maids.[27] "The study's key revelation was simple, but profound: **Our expectations shape our outcomes**. "This turns out to be a good summary of one of the most influential discoveries psychologists have made in the past fifty years—that how we think about something affects how it is."[28] I'll put it another way: **Our mindsets shape our outcomes.**

If we believe something will have positive results, it will generate change. This is why it is so important to have a growth mindset. When the maids viewed their work as exercise, they experienced a growth mindset. They got healthier by making a paradigm shift. They viewed their work with different eyes. Nothing else changed about their circumstances. They did the same work each day. But their mindset about their work changed and produced positive results in their health.

A growth mindset changes the rules of engagement. Thoughts of growth generate healthier, confident minds. The way to know when we've experienced a paradigm shift and entered a new mindset is when we allow ourselves room to learn and grow. Becoming whole is better than being broken.[29] We see things differently. The maids believed their work was exercise and this new belief produced positive results. Mindfulness is powerful.

Charles Duhigg writes, in his book, *The Power of Habits*, "If you believe you can change—if you make it a habit—the change becomes real. This is the real power of habit: the insight that your habits are what you choose them to be. Once that choice occurs—and becomes automatic—it's not only real, it starts to seem inevitable . . . "[30] (More on how to make the growth mindset a habit comes later in this book.) For now, let's keep pushing the idea of a mindset shift. Let's continue to open the world of possibility around us.

We are always quick to measure our success or our lack of success within the world of measurements.[31] But entering a new mindset changes the rules. Take the nine-dot puzzle. It's a mathematical puzzle whose task is to connect nine squarely arranged points with a pen by four (or fewer) straight lines without lifting the pen. Give it a try.

Nearly everybody completes the task like this:

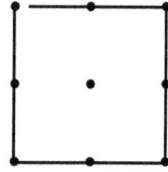

FIXED MINDSET

Most draw a square because they hear, "Connect the dots with four straight lines without taking pen from paper," and they see only a square. But it doesn't solve the puzzle. The puzzle seems impossible until we realize we can solve it by extending the lines past the border of dots. Gary Klein writes, "(Seeing a square) creates an impasse because we make natural assumptions that turn out to be inappropriate for the task. We assume that we are supposed to stay within the borders."[32] The phrase "thinking outside the box"comes from this solution strategy.

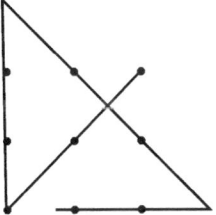

GROWTH MINDSET

Being in a fixed mindset works like this puzzle, doesn't it? We think we are in a box, at a dead end, not capable of getting out. But when we enter a new mindset, we enter a new world. We see the correct rules of engagement. We see the open space of possibility. We think "outside the box."

Our expectations shape our outcomes. Take this experiment with milkshakes.

Alia Crum and her associates conducted a study on two separate occasions, where participants consumed a 380-calorie milkshake under the pretense that it was either a 620-calorie "indulgent" shake or a 140-calorie "sensible" shake[33]. When the participants thought they were drinking the indulgent milkshake with 620-calories, they produced less of a gut peptide that stimulates hunger. The mindset of indulgence produced a dramatically steeper decline in ghrelin after consuming the shake, whereas the mindset of sensibility produced a relatively flat ghrelin response. Participants' satiety was consistent with what they believed they were consuming rather than the actual nutritional value of what they consumed. Alia Crum concluded that beliefs changed their body's physical reaction to the very same drink. Mindset meaningfully affects physiological responses to food.

What we expect matters. Expect guilt and condemnation and you will feel its bondage. Expect grace and you will experience the freedom of possibility. So I will leave you with a question: What is possible for you?

REFLECTIONS

1. Do you feel trapped in a box that you can't get out?

2. List two ways having a growth mindset will change your circumstances.

THE SYSTEM BEHIND THE CURTAIN

*And I can change. I can live out of my imagination
instead of my memory. I can tie myself to my
limitless potential instead of my limiting past.*

—STEPHEN R. COVEY

In 1946 Perry Spencer, a grammar school dropout and an electronic genius, was working in front of a magnetron, the power tube that drives radar. As he stood there, he noticed a candy bar in his pocket began to melt. He reflected on it and thought it was strange that his candy bar started melting for no reason. Being an inquisitive person, he took the next logical step and held a bag of popcorn in front of the magnetron. To his amazement, the kernels popped. All of this led to one of the greatest inventions of all time—the microwave. Most of us would have only been annoyed and complained about our melted candy bar melting.

Reflective thought led to the invention of the microwave. It makes us wonder just how many inventions are going undiscovered in the world. Most of us are running on autopilot, hardly ever reflecting on our lives. It's easy to get bogged down in the minutiae of everyday life and fail to notice important opportunities for change. Most of our choices are being made automatically. Professor Wendy Wood says, "In research that I've done, we find that about 43% of what people do every day is repeated in the same context, usually while they are thinking about something else. They're automatically responding without really making decisions."[34]

We don't give habits much thought. Katy Milkman writes, "As habits develop, we rely less and less on the parts of our brain that are used for reasoning, the prefrontal cortex, and more and more on the parts that are responsible for action and motor control."[35] Sounds like we have two brains and in a way, we do. Let's see how it works.

To get at this idea of two systems in the brain, let me tell you a story about a famous organist back in the 1800's. This organist would travel from town to town giving concerts. These were days when someone had to work behind the scenes to pump the organ while the musician played the keys, so in each place the organist hired a boy to pump the organ during the concert.

In one town, he hired a precocious boy who continued to hang around with him even afterward. He couldn't shake the boy, who followed him to his hotel one night and said, "We sure had us a great concert tonight, didn't we?" "What do you mean *we*?" said the famous organist. "*I* had a great concert. There is no *we*. There is only *I*. Now why don't you go home?" So, the boy went home.

The next night, though, when the organist was halfway through a magnificent fugue, the organ suddenly stopped. It gave a little groan, then just quit. The organist continued to play for a few seconds, but there was absolutely no sound. He was stupefied and didn't know what to do; nothing like this had ever happened before. What could possibly be wrong?

Just then the little boy stuck his head around the corner, grinned, and said, "*We* aren't having a very good concert tonight, are *we*?"

The brain is like the famous organist and the boy. One part of our brain runs things behind the scenes—never sticking its head out from behind the curtain—while the other performs on the stage. And both need each other. The Nobel Prize winner, Daniel Kahneman calls these two functions in the brain, the Automatic System and Reflective System,[36] which respectively produce fast and slow thinking. He writes, "I speak of the features of intuitive and deliberate thought as

if they were traits and dispositions of two characters in your mind."[37]
He believes the Automatic System operates automatically and quickly,
with little or no effort and no sense of voluntary control. The Reflective
System is the conscious, reasoning self that makes choices and decides
what to think and what to do. The Reflective System believes, like the
organist, that it is the star of the show. But the Automatic System, like
the boy behind the curtain, produces the power behind the scenes. It's
where our habits are formed.

The key features of each system are shown in the table[38] below:

TABLE 1

TWO COGNITIVE SYSTEMS

AUTOMATIC SYSTEM	REFLECTIVE SYSTEM
Uncontrolled	Controlled
Effortless	Effortful
Associative	Deductive
Fast	Slow
Unconsicous	Self-aware
Skilled	Rule-following

(Note. From Richard Thaler & Cass Sunstein, *Nudge: Improving Decisions About Health, Wealth, and Happiness*, 20. Copyright 2008 by Yale University Press.)

The Automatic System is rapid and instinctive. It does not involve
what we usually associate with thinking. When you duck because a
ball is thrown at you unexpectedly, or get nervous when your airplane
hits turbulence, you are using your Automatic System. The Reflective
System is more deliberate and self-conscious. It's the part of our brain
we use when doing math or deciding on what route to take on a trip.[39]

I mention these two systems because transformation occurs when
we change the Automatic System's autopilot settings. This is how
we renew the mind (Romans 12:2). The renewing takes place in the

Automatic System and is therefore much harder to control because it runs on an internal model.

Our Automatic System is the secret author of many of the choices and judgments we make.[40] It is the power behind the curtain of consciousness. It is where change needs to occur.

Kahneman writes, "The (Reflective System) has some ability to change the way the (Automatic System) works, by programming the normally automatic functions of attention and memory."[41] This is good news because this is the way we are going to empty-out the old patterns and change our bad habits. We will do this by reprogramming the Automatic System that is running our habits and automatic thoughts. So, how does this work?

AUTOMATIC SYSTEM
Fast, unconscious, able to handle many processes at the same time, bundles things together that seem similar, and consumes little energy

REFLECTIVE SYSTEM
Slow, conscious, only one process can take place at any time, analytic and consumes a lot of energy

PAYING ATTENTION

The Reflective System oversees self-control.[42] The Reflective System controls this impulse from the Automatic System. It catches the thought and stops it. This is huge to know when we are wanting to change our habits. Charles Duhigg writes, in his book, *The Power of Habit,* "When a habit emerges, the brain stops fully participating in decision making. It stops working so hard, or diverts focus to other tasks. So unless you deliberately fight a habit—unless you find new routines—the pattern will unfold automatically."[43] This happens because our minds are always looking for ways to reduce energy. It's the path of least resistance. This is why we have the Automatic System. We would go crazy if we had to consciously think of everything we do, so stopping and analyzing the Automatic System takes effort and attention. It's not easy.

It takes work to change unwanted habits and behavior, because the behavior has become easy and automatic. That's why the Reflective System likes a habit. But to change a habit, I must make a decision to break the habit. I must stop and take control of autopilot. We could call it paying attention. Curt Thompson writes, "I tell my patients that one of the most important questions they can reflect on is the following: **How well am I paying attention to what I'm paying attention to?"[44]**

In my life, it goes back to the roots of my car wreck. Paying attention to why I felt fear and insecurity allowed me to break its script. Today, let's start this process by paying attention to what we should be paying attention to. Take Portia Nelson's poem, *An Autobiography in Five Chapters* as an example of how the process of self-awareness occurs:

Chapter 1.

I walked down the street. There is a deep hole in the sidewalk. I fall in. I am lost. I am helpless. It isn't my fault. It takes forever to find a way out.

Chapter 2.

I walked down the street. There is a deep hole in the sidewalk. I pretend I don't see it. I fall in again. I can't believe I'm in the same place, but it isn't my fault. It still takes a long time to get out.

Chapter 3.

I walked down the street. There is a deep hole in the sidewalk. I see it is there. I still fall in. It's a habit. My eyes are open. I know where I am. It is my fault. I get out immediately.

Chapter 4.

I walk down the same street. There is a deep hole in the sidewalk. I walk around it.

Chapter 5.

I walk down another street.[45]

It takes self-awareness to recognize unwanted habits. We must pay attention to what thoughts are dictating our behavior. Running on autopilot is how we keep traveling the same street and falling into the same deep hole. But when we see the hole for what it is—something to be decided on and avoided—it stops the Automatic System and brings the Reflective System online to break the habit.

The Reflective System is in charge of doubting and unbelieving what's in the Automatic System.[46] More on this later. For now, start training yourself to pay attention to why you are automatically doing certain things. Become mindful of unwanted habits, the way the maids became mindful of their work being fitness. Recognize how your emotions, your thoughts, and your behavior are all connected and wired in your brain. **Nothing changes without attention and effort.** This is why the apostle Paul wrote, "We demolish arguments and every pretension that sets itself up against the knowledge of God, and we take captive every thought to make it obedient to Christ" (2 Corinthians 10:5).

Dr. Caroline Leaf writes, "Neurons that don't get enough signal (the rehearsing of the negative event) will start firing apart, wiring apart, pulling out, and destroying the emotion attached to the trauma."[47] Pruning our thoughts and breaking free from bad habits is how the Reflective System changes the Automatic System's toxic autopilot settings. It works by capturing our thoughts and replacing them with higher thoughts. If we keep thinking the same thoughts, we experience the same results. We never change streets. We keep falling in the same deep hole.

REFLECTION

1. How do you capture a thought?

2. In Portia Nelson's *Autobiography in Five Short Chapters*, what chapter is your life in at this moment—1, 2, 3, 4 or 5?

RENEWING THE ATTITUDES OF OUR MIND

Hope confronts. It does not ignore pain, agony, or injustice.
It is not a saccharine optimism that refuses to see, face, or grapple
with the wretchedness of reality. You can't have hope without despair,
because hope is a response. Hope is the active conviction
that despair will never have the last word.

—CORY BOOKER

Faith the dog was born without forelimbs. From puppyhood, she's been able to walk on her two hind legs, bipedally, like a human. She demonstrates how our brains can adapt and free us from circumstances. She had a growth mindset. Her drive for survival allowed the flexible circuitry in her brain to try out many hypotheses and solve the problem, so she could achieve her goals of food, shelter, and care. She found a way—when there seemed to be no way. Neuroscientist David Eagleman writes about Faith the dog, "A brain's goals play a critical role in how and when it changes. Brains learn to control whatever body plan they discover themselves inside of."[48]

Brains respond to rewarded goals. Faith the dog had goals—sustenance and love—and her mind accommodated them. She figured out how to work her body in these parameters, because the brain is extremely clever at using context to know what programs to run. We do the same thing. "(Our brain) employs a schema (patterns to organize different categories of information) such that when you are on a bicycle, you transport yourself by moving your thighs in circles, but while jogging, you swing your arms and lift your feet to step over things in the road."[49] So context tells the brain which schema to run.

The question becomes: Can we get inside our minds and fiddle with the gears and change schemas? Just think if Faith the dog had just accepted her schema of not being able to walk on her two hind feet. She would have lived a helpless life. But, as we will see in week two of our study, when habits and goals are in line, they smoothly integrate to guide our actions,[50] the way Faith the dog's goals guided her into a new life.

For this reason, Paul writes, "You were taught, with regard to your former way of life, to put off your *old self*, which is being corrupted by its deceitful desires; to be made new in the attitude of your minds; and to put on the new self, created to be like God in true righteousness and holiness" (Ephesians 4:22–24). The old self (and its deceitful desires) is not indicative of the *new self*. To put off (apothesthai) means to renounce. This is more than behavior change. The old self is corrupt and is no longer working for us. We need a new way of thinking that will form new schemas for the new self.

OLD SELF
Who we once were, does not determine who we are today.

NEW SELF
Who we are becoming. We see things in a new way.

You could say that the patterns of this world are the habits we've formed under the old self and to put off the old self we will need to break habits and form new ones. These old habits are rooted in pride, insecurity, doubt, fear, the approval of others, and shame—the patterns of this world.

Transformation means a new schema with new habits. The old is gone, the new is here. Putting on the new self will feel as awkward as walking on our hands. But this is what the kingdom of God is asking us to do. Jesus said the kingdom of God is an upside-down kingdom. The first shall be last, the last shall be first (Matthew 20:16). Whoever wants to be the most important must be last of all and servant of all. (Mark 9:35). The context of the kingdom of God runs from different patterns. Everything is being turned upside-down. The success of the world is no longer our schema. We operate on the concepts of the kingdom.

Renewing our minds allows us to run a different schema. ". . . we no longer conform to the patterns of this world" (Romans 12:2). We adopt new patterns (habits). We run a different schema. When we create a habit, we create new neural pathways. This gets at the heart of transformation. This is why habits are so powerful. They are automatic and form the basis of our patterns. And our new schema with new habits will come more evident as we move through our time together. So, let's keep working on the elements of a paradigm shift, then we will move onto habit formation in week two.

SEEING THE ROOM

As cognitive psychology professor Jordan Peterson puts it: "There's an infinite wealth of information in this room, yet when you come in and you process it, you only see those things that directly serve your purposes. The things you don't know and the territories you don't know how to maneuver in, are everywhere."[51] This is what Faith the dog faced when trying to figure out how to maneuver in this world. There were things she didn't know, but she didn't rest inside a fixed mindset of helplessness. She transformed her life by understanding that she could grow and learn how to step into these territories. She understood a paradigm shift of adopting a growth mindset.

When we talk about experiencing a paradigm shift from a fixed mindset to a growth mindset, then we are talking about seeing the new possibilities of these unseen territories and figuring out—like Faith the dog—how to maneuver in them to obtain what we desire. We learn what we need to know. "We walk by faith and not by sight" (2 Corinthians 5:7).

We create the values in this new context, which alters behavior. Expected rewards or expected consequences guide our future actions. But it's more than behavior modification. Jesus could have just told us to be better. He didn't have to die if it's all about behavior. It's not. It's about transformation from the old self to the new self. It's a total revolution of mind, soul, and body.

The Russian writer Leo Tolstoy described this aspect of personal change in his book, *My Religion*, which chronicles his religious transformation and details the mindset with which he subsequently came to view the world:

> "For thirty-five years of my life, I was . . . a man who believed in nothing. Five years ago faith came to me . . . and my whole life underwent a sudden transformation . . . What had once appeared to me right now became wrong and the wrong of the past I beheld as right . . . My life and my desires were completely changed; good and evil interchanged meanings."[52]

His self-concept changed. Studies have proven that "when talking about their pre-changed lives, changed people appear not to focus on their past environment or on reliving their past reactions; changed people seem to focus on their discrepant past selves instead."[53] Isn't this Tolstoy's point?

Imagine if Faith the dog could tell us about her past self being unable to walk on her hind feet. How would she describe it? "In my former way of life, crawling on my belly . . . " Her mind would never reconfigure and conform to the past. She would never return to her former way of life and be overcome by the urge to crawl on her belly again. Her cognitive framework has changed to meet her body context. Once she understood walking on her hind feet was possible, her brain rewired itself. She built new neural pathways. Eagleman writes, "Thinking a thought is like moving a limb; in the same way that our brains drive a kick, a lunge, or a grasp, it may be that thinking moves concepts around in thought space."[54] We can control our concepts. The attitude of our mind is a movable and transformative construct that can create new realities and change our mindset from being broken (fixed) to becoming whole (growth). It's a dividing line. We renounce one and accept the other. Therefore, we can never say our past is part of our future. The old is gone, the new has come. A belief that we have changed is a belief that we will cause us to act differently from how we acted in the past. Stephen Covey writes, "Self-awareness enables us to stand apart and examine even the way we 'see' ourselves—our self-paradigm, the most fundamental paradigm of effectiveness."[55]

HOW A WALLPAPER CLEANER BECAME A CHILD'S TOY

In the early part of the 20th century, Kutol Products was the largest wallpaper cleaner manufacturer in the world. Founded in 1912 in Cincinnati, Ohio, the company sold a soft, pliable, nontoxic compound used for wiping soot from wallpaper. And this soot was a huge problem for households in those days. But in the 1950s, America transitioned from dirtier coal to cleaner oil, gas, and electricity, which meant that sooty build-up on wallpaper was no longer an issue, causing sales to plummet, which put the company on the brink of bankruptcy.

Then someone at Kutol read a newspaper article about how their wallpaper cleaner was being used for modeling projects, so they tested the nontoxic compound with children. The results were amazing. Kids loved modeling it into all kinds of shapes. So, they gave it a new name: Play-Doh. And Play-Doh has "sold more than 3 billion cans since its debut as a child's toy in 1956—eclipsing its previous existence as a wallpaper cleaner by light years."[56] What was once a wallpaper cleaner became a toy in the hands of a child.

Becoming a new creation changes our purpose. Kutol rescripted the use and message of a wallpaper cleaner. They reshaped, reformed, repurposed a wallpaper cleaner and created something new, Play-Doh. A simple way to look at this is to always refer to your former self in the third person. The old self is "not me." Play-Doh would say, "The old wallpaper cleaner is not me."

Studies have shown that the "not me" perspective suggests we see our past self from the vantage point of looking at another person.[57] By stepping outside ourselves, we gain perspective. Psychologist Robert Kegan, chair of adult development at Harvard, argues that the single most important move we can make to accelerate personal growth is to adopt a "subject-object shift," which means our subjective selves—who we think we are—should shift to having objective distance. "And when we can move from being subject to our identity to having some objective distance from it, we gain flexibility in how we respond to life and its challenges."[58] We lose ourselves to find ourselves (Luke 17:33). We step outside of our heads to gain a new perspective. We dethrone the ego by becoming its observer.

EGO
Our identity, who we believe we are. It encompasses all of our fears, our insecurities, our doubts, as well as what leads us to believe we're better than or inferior to other people.

Growth mindsets depend on perception changes that take on the third-person perspective. There's a psychological disconnect between past and present—our paradigm shifts. Dr. Joe Dispenza writes, "So if we want to change some aspect of our reality, we have to think, feel, and act in new ways; we have to 'be' different in terms of our responses to experiences. We have to 'become' someone else. We have to create a new state of mind . . . we need to observe a new outcome with that new mind."[59]

Invoking the notion of an old self when describing past behavior implies that the old self actively determined that behavior. We were not simply forced to behave that way by external forces. By attributing past behavior to this old self means that it's not indicative of who we are today. Transforming our minds into a new way of being and seeing is how we become who God keeps insisting we are. This is true identity change. Faith the dog can never go back to crawling on her belly. The spirit of her mind has transformed her body. This is Paul's reasoning when he tells us we need to be made new in the attitude of our minds (Ephesians 4:22-25). What changes is the spirit of our mind. We think in a different way. We look at, meditate about, cogitate concerning, precisely the same data, but we do not see the same thing in the same way. The spirit of our mind is changed. Our outlook is completely new.[60]

Once we understand our new relationship with Christ, a paradigm of growth emerges. The whole way we think changes the attitude of the mind. Faith the dog used her mind to change the way her body performed. She had to learn how to maneuver in a world that wasn't made for her body. She had to go against what felt natural. She had to detach. Adam Grant, in his book, *Think Again: The Power of Knowing What You Don't Know,* writes, "I've learned that two kinds of detachment are especially useful: detaching your present from your past and detaching your opinions from your identity . . . In one study, when people felt detached from their past selves, they became less depressed over the course of the year. When you feel as if your life is changing direction and you're in the process of shifting who you are, it's easier to walk away from foolish beliefs you once held."[61]

Until the past becomes the past, then nothing changes. But if you can visualize your past from a third-person perspective, then you've changed your paradigm and will relive less pain of the old self. A self-concept (identity) change is a cognitive framework change. James Clear writes:

> "Most people don't even consider identity change when they set out to improve. They just think, "I want to be skinny (outcome) and if I stick to this diet, then I'll be

skinny (process)." They set goals and determine the actions they should take to achieve those goals without considering the beliefs that drive their actions. They never shift the way they look at themselves and they don't realize that their old identity can sabotage their new plans for change."[62]

Again, think of Kutol. What if the new label for Play-Doh included an alternative use as a wallpaper cleaner. There would be confusion. One use had to remain and one use had to go to create the new identity. This is why a psychological disconnect from our old self is so important. This is why Paul called it "putting off the old self."

Okay, I hear you say, "What if we've made mistakes along the way after putting on the new self?" Something I read by Richard Rohr is appropriate here: "Before transformation, sin is any kind of moral mistake; afterward, sin is a mistake about who you are and whose you are."[63]

REFLECTIONS

1. Write a paragraph describing your past self. What are you leaving behind?

2. Now write a paragraph about your new self. What do you want your new identity to look like? What are your new goals?

HABIT FORMATION

THE KEY TO HABIT CHANGE

Habits are first cobwebs, then cables.

—Spanish proverb

How many times have you vowed to break a bad habit but haven't? How many diets have you tried over the years? How many times have you made New Year's resolutions and broken them? How many times have you said "no" to something detrimental to your soul, only to end up doing it again? How many gyms have you joined in the last ten years? Every self-improvement program must discuss habits and habit formation because willpower alone never works. Research proves it.

Studies have proven that most dieters eventually fall back into their old eating and exercising patterns. "Five years after taking part in a typical weight-loss program, only about 15% of participants have kept off even ten pounds. The vast majority are back to their original weight, or have even gained more."[64] Why is this the case? Habits are hard to break and most people think willpower and persistence will do the trick. But habits are rooted in the Automatic System and run under the hood of consciousness. This makes them hard to detect and change. They no longer need the Reflective System to exist. As we've seen, the Automatic System and the Reflective System run on two different wavelengths. And habits work without our conscious control of them.

This is how 43% of what drives our behavior each day is a result of our habits.[65] It's all-automatic and unconscious.

Most Americans believe lack of individual willpower is the biggest barrier to weight loss.[66] We believe we are in charge of free will. We believe we chose the bad habit, now we can change it with willpower and persistence. But is this true? Is willpower the problem? Let's take a look at how we form habits to get an understanding of willpower and transformation.

THE POWER OF HABIT

To illustrate how we form habits, Charles Duhigg, in his book *The Power of Habit,* tells a story about Claude C. Hopkins a prominent American executive in the early 1900s. Hopkins was approached by an old friend who had discovered an amazing product—toothpaste. His friend told him that it would be a hit if Hopkins could only help design a national promotional campaign. This was Hopkins' expertise. He had seduced millions of women into purchasing Palmolive soap by proclaiming Cleopatra had washed with it, despite the protests of outraged historians. Hopkins knew the right human psychology to sell products. He had learned two basic rules:

First, find a simple and obvious cue.

Second, clearly define the rewards.

But Hopkins wasn't sure he could create magic for a toothpaste campaign. He felt he had nothing to sell the public on concerning the benefits of brushing their teeth. At that time only 7% of Americans had a tube of toothpaste.

One day while combing through dental textbooks, he discovered tooth film. We all know the feeling of running our tongue along our teeth and feeling that film, and he knew he had the first part of his advertising campaign magic. He only had to make people aware of the tooth film and the benefits of brushing it away. Then the reward would be having beautiful teeth. By using this cue (tooth film) and reward (beautiful teeth), he persuaded millions to start a daily ritual of brushing. But what Hopkins missed was a third rule of habit formation that we now understand as *neurological cravings*.[67] These cravings emerge so gradually that we're not even aware they exist. This is how the Automatic System gets involved in habit formation. When our brain starts expecting the reward—craving the endorphins or a sense of accomplishment—then it becomes automatic to lace up our jogging shoes for a run.[68] All is well when we are succeeding and meeting our desired goal. But what happens when we attempt to change bad habits? Then our "conscious decision-making self is pitted against our habitual, automatic responses. We are wrenched over and over by bad habits, in a sort of internal war."[69] Paul describes this battle in Romans 7.

NEUROLOGICAL CRAVINGS
Unconscious expectation or craving for a reward.

WHAT ARE HABITS?

Habits are repeated actions in the same context that receive a reward. They become mental shortcuts that get encoded in our *habit memory system* in the brain. Habit formation needs three elements:

1. **Repetition**—a habit needs repetition on a regular basis, in the same way. If we want to improve fitness, we go to a gym on a regular basis and repeat a certain exercise regimen.

2. **Rewards**—we repeat what gets rewarded, so we do what we enjoy. Make behavior fun.

3. **Context**—habits are cued by the context we are in. A performance context is what surrounds us when we do something. So, we need a stable context. Free of stress.[70]

Performing these three elements encodes behavior in the habit memory system and habits in the brain never really disappear. This is good and bad. Think of riding a bike or lacing up your shoes. But when it comes to forming new habits, the one we want to change doesn't vanish with our decision to do something better for our lives and loved ones. As soon as our willpower wanes, old habits resurface with a vengeance.[71] So habit formation can be a good thing or a bad thing. The problem with the brain is that it doesn't know a good habit from a bad one.[72] It's only looking to reduce energy and save itself from having to deal with constant conflict resolution. This leads us to repetition. Repetition creates a favorable mental condition that makes things run smoothly. So, let's look at the individual elements of habit formation.

HABIT MEMORY SYSTEM
Gradual acquisition of associations between stimuli and responses, such as learning to make one choice rather than another.

REPETITION

Repetition is showing up for the hard work to form a better habit. We must be somewhat consistent. And consistency is more than willpower. It's a commitment to making life better, no matter how many reps it takes to get there. So, the question becomes: how long does it take to form a new habit? Studies have shown that it takes ninety-one days for an exercise routine to become habitual, meaning we no longer make a decision on the action. We just perform it automatically without thinking about it.[73]

Maybe you've heard that it takes twenty-one days to turn an action into a habit. This is a myth based on an old self-help book from the 1960s. The author guessed how long it took people to adjust to self-changes—such as plastic surgery—and came up with the twenty-one-day period. But habit formation depends on the new action we are trying to automate.

The sweet spot of habit formation is when we feel that the repetition of the action has become automated. We just lace up our tennis shoes for the run without thinking about the energy it will take or even the endorphin high. Our desired action no longer creates conflict resolution. We are no longer weighing our options to run or to remain on the couch for one more episode of our favorite TV show. We are lacing up our shoes with no conflict. Then, "after a while, conflict resolution starts to favor the new behavior . . . processing speed is the reason. Habits come to mind quickly."[74] So, repetition is doing an action until it hits the sweet spot of automation.

REWARDS

After a preacher died and went to heaven, he noticed that a New York cab driver had been given a higher place than he had. "I don't understand," he complained to St. Peter. "I devoted my entire life to my congregation."

"Our policy is to reward results," explained St. Peter. "Now what happened, Reverend, whenever you gave a sermon?"

The minister admitted that some in the congregation fell asleep.

"Exactly," said St. Peter. "And when people rode in this man's taxi, they not only stayed awake, but they also prayed."

Heaven tends to be the place where we are rewarded for the deeds we've accomplished on earth. Jesus said, "Great is your reward in heaven" (Matthew 5:12). So, there is a sense that rewards are important. Not only do they spur us on toward heaven, but they also work in the brain by producing acetylcholine. "Acetylcholine broadcasts widely throughout the brain and as a result it can trigger changes with any kind of relevant stimulus, whether a musical note, a texture, or a verbal accolade. Acetylcholine is a universal mechanism for saying, "this is important—get better at detecting this." It makes relevance by increasing territory."[75] It turns on brain plasticity—the process that causes our brains to change and grow.

Healthy rewards are built on what we value (relevance), because what we value, we reward. Stephen Covey writes, "Proactive people are still influenced by external stimuli, whether physical, social, or psychological. But their response to the stimuli, conscious or unconscious, is a value-based choice or response."[76] We must value the reward. Studies have proven that when reward is withheld, our brains disengage.[77] The brain basically says, "Why should I give energy to something that doesn't reward my effort?" So, a habit never fully forms if the brain loses interest. Also, if the habit doesn't become automatic in our unconscious, then it doesn't get encoded in our habit memory system. Rewards make sure the brain is engaged until habits are formed, then rewards aren't needed anymore.

Dr. David Eagleman describes this process by telling us to imagine an F-sharp note being played for us on a piano. The note triggers activity in our auditory cortex, but it doesn't change anything about how much territory is devoted to F-sharp in that region of the brain. Why not? Because the note means nothing in particular to us. Now imagine each time he plays the note, he gives us a warm chocolate chip cookie. In this case the note accrues—and the territory devoted to F-sharp expands. Your brain assigns more ground to that frequency because the presence of reward indicates that it must be important.[78] So our brains respond to rewards on a deep level. Now the habit has its own territory in the habit memory system. It's all automatic and below consciousness. And we don't even need the chocolate chip cookie anymore.

Once habits are formed, rewards don't make a whole lot of difference. If you change the context, will people keep performing the habit? If you change the reward, will people keep doing it? Wendy Wood says this is the gold-standard of whether something is a habit or not.[79] Without the context and without the reward, would you still perform the act? If you answer yes to both, then you have a deeply, ingrained habit. This is why it is so hard to change habits. They no longer need our conscious awareness to exist. We just mindlessly act.

CONTEXT

Context cues our habits. It's what surrounds us when we are repeating an action. And the context should be stable, or the habit will never form. Habits hate change. They are like hermits looking for a safe place to thrive. We must arrange our lives to reliably and unfailingly cue our new desired habit. Wendy Wood writes, "Only by keeping your life as consistent as possible will your habit grow. Otherwise, you can expect it to develop slowly, like a plant with far too little light."[80]

Context creates this consistency. If we keep changing our context cues, we can't just act out of habit. We must stop and make decisions. The Reflective System interrupts the formation of habits, as we will learn more about later, so for now just know that context plays a huge role in habit formation. And context isn't just a "physical environment." Our context can also consist of intangible things: the time of day or our state of mind.

MAKING THE UNCONSCIOUS CONSCIOUS

Carl Jung once said, "Until you make the unconscious conscious, it will direct your life and you will call it fate." The habits we give territory to in the brain grow tentacles so deep we end up becoming unwilling victims to their stronghold—without even knowing it controls us. So, capturing our thoughts wakes the brain up. Then plasticity creates new neural networks for the habits we value. Much like the F-sharp note we discussed earlier. New territory in the brain emerges to house these new habits. As a result, strongholds (bad habits) are demolished.

We must get good at recognizing when the brain wakes up and pays attention. Have you ever had a feeling that you shrugged off, but later realized it was a precious moment of possibility that you missed because you ignored it? This is what I'm asking of you—pay attention to relevance in the brain. We can't experience a paradigm shift until we uncover the habits that are controlling 43% of what we do daily. This is how we get the Reflective System involved. It is in charge of doubting and unbelieving what's in the Automatic System.[81] Socrates said, "Awareness of ignorance is the beginning of wisdom." Let's keep looking for ways to uncover unwanted habits.

REFLECTIONS:

1. Have any unwanted habits emerged from your unconscious after reading this chapter?

2. Can you list some of your core values? What matters most to you?

3. Now list some ways that you can make what you value into new habits.

HOW TO BE A CHOICE ARCHITECT

When you have to make a choice and don't make it,
that is in itself a choice.

—WILLIAM JAMES

We've all witnessed a child's meltdown. Maybe even experienced a very public one. It's a very embarrassing situation for a parent. All a parent can do is give in or holdout. Sometimes parents give in. The pressure becomes too much in the checkout aisle. The glares and stares of other customers are overwhelming as their child has a meltdown over some impulse item placed there by a choice architect to provoke children to want and for parents to buy. Scenes like this play out in stores all over America because we are being manipulated. Someone is behind this manipulation and that someone is a choice architect.

"A choice architect has the responsibility for organizing the context in which people make decisions."[82] Retail space is their manipulative playground. They are trying to motivate you to choose certain things. They've lined certain areas with candy and other impulse choices that make children literally meltdown under the pressure. But children are not the only target.

Did you know that almost all of us turn to the right after entering a store? (Think about it the next time you enter a store.) Retailers have viewed thousands of hours of videotapes showing shoppers turning right once they clear the front doors. So, retailers position their most profitable products on the right side, hoping you'll buy them. Also, consider cereal and soups: when they are shelved out of alphabetical order and seemingly at random, our instinct is to linger a bit longer and look at a wider selection, which could tempt us to grab an extra box of another brand.[83]

These days it has gotten even easier for retailers to track our buying habits and place us inside the context of the choice architect. We are being influenced. This is why fruits and vegetables are up front in a grocery store. They hope your Automatic System will have a little more authority by the time you get to the sweet stuff, because your Reflective System has made some good choices by this point. All of us have walked out of the grocery store loaded down with things we didn't really need. All because we let our Automatic Systems do the deciding within the context of temptation. Everywhere we go, the influences of the world's systems are designed to aim our thoughts and our decisions. So not being influenced by the world's system is the battle. This is the renewing of the mind—no longer conforming to the patterns of this world.

BUILDING A BETTER SYSTEM

Let's say that we decided our child's recent meltdown in the checkout aisle would be their last. How could we arrange things so that the temptation would be neutralized? The answer seems easy enough. We have two options. We can avoid the store or turn their desire for candy into a reward. Let's say they clean their room and we promise to reward them at the grocery store with one candy item. Now the impulse is no longer a sudden meltdown. It's a reward. Of course, it doesn't have to be candy. Just a reward of some kind. Neuroscientist David Eagleman writes, "An important technique is to train (children) to pause and consider the future outcome of any choice they might make—encouraging them to run simulations of what might happen—thereby strengthening neural connections that can override the immediate gratification of impulses."[84] Now we have created an if-then plan to prevent a meltdown.

By setting up this reward in advance, we control the craving and the craving is why our children have a meltdown. Once we control their reward, their behavior in the grocery store line is not due to a craving, but the result of creating a system to neutralize the temptation. Once the reward has been encoded, the craving is satisfied. Remember, habits are rewards realized. Rewarded responses are repeated in the brain. It's just like receiving that chocolate chip cookie when we hear the F-sharp note. The presence of a reward creates more room in the auditory cortex.

CREATING A SYSTEM FOR OUR HABITS

James Clear writes, "If you want better results, then forget about setting goals. Focus on your system instead."[85] If we can create an automated system to make the right choices between stimulus and response, then you will no longer need to have deliberate thoughts from the Reflective System. This is the context change I mentioned about Faith the dog. We reset the system by putting on the new self. Now we've fiddled with the gears under the hood. We've integrated our own habit system that will run and make wise choices. Because when we act out of habit without having to make a decision to do so, we create new neural pathways and a whole new way of life.

THE BURDEN OF RELIGION

In traditional religion, the old self is dependent upon the righteousness of works. We work our way to heaven by behavior modification. Repeated rewards of looking good for others, the repeated rewards of wealth, of fame, of power are what Paul calls the deceitful desires (Ephesians 4:22). These are not the rewards of being the new creation, so any bad habit is one that's not in correlation with the new creation.

For example, Jesus pointed out that the Father feeds the birds, then he told His audience that the Father cares much more for us. So don't worry. Worrying doesn't correlate with the new creation. Trusting does. Worrying is a bad habit. Trusting God is a good habit. Our actions should flow from being the new creation.

Think of Christ as the choice architect. It's much like the man sorting oranges I told you about on Day 3. A choice architect set up a system for the man to make sure he was making wise decisions. Small holes for small oranges. Large holes for large oranges. Another hole for bruised ones. This is a choice architect at their best. They have designed the system for the worker to make decisions.

Maybe the most famous architect comes from Greek mythology. In Homer's, *The Odyssey*[86] and Virgil's *Aeneid*, the legendary hero Odysseus also known by the Latin variant Ulysses realized his ship would soon be passing an island where the beautiful sirens lived. The sirens were famous for singing songs so melodious that sailors were rapt and enchanted. The sirens' songs were so irresistible, the bewitched sailors would be drawn into the rocky shore until their ships crashed and the sirens would plunder their treasure. So Ulysses had his men tie him to the mast. He then told his men under no conditions were they to untie him and told them to fill their ears with wax. They made it past the island of sirens. Ulysses created a controlled context that predicted an outcome.

Ulysses knew that his future self would be in no position to make good decisions. The Ulysses of sound mind orchestrated the environment to guide his decisions, deliberately introducing obstacles and making it more challenging to yield to temptation. He anchored himself to the mast of behavior modification, ensuring he couldn't be drawn off course by the siren's call. You will see this system in most of the books on habit formation and even in religious books when they tell us to make sin look unattractive. But where the Christian stands apart is how we don't focus on behavior, but focus on being the new creation. Jesus put it like this: "Take my yoke upon you and learn from me, for I am gentle and humble in heart and you will find rest for your souls" (Matthew 11:29). The system of the new creation is taking on the yoke or burden of a gentle and humble Christ. But those who labor and are heavy–burdened are those who are sighing under the yoke of the religious law in thought and in actions.[87] Religion is the instinct to do something to be accepted. But the yoke of Christ is grace that brings rest. I end my striving and vying for the world's recognition.

Creating the system of grace is more than behavior modification. It's a paradigm. It's a lens. It's our way of seeing the world through a mindset of grace. We believe Christ is dwelling within us, that we are together, that we are one. The old state of things has passed away. Now there is a new state of things. Behavior modification based on religion doesn't produce this new creation. This is Paul's point in Galatians 6:15: "Neither circumcision nor uncircumcision means anything; what counts is the new creation." Inside this paradigm we find that the will of God is a good thing. We begin to like the will of God and begin to desire it. We've transformed the attitude of our minds, changing the direction of our thoughts.

Now you talk about a different paradigm. The mindset of grace is the most powerful system in the world. We discover in this system that God's will is pleasing and perfect. How is it pleasing? It rewards us, not with happiness, but with righteousness, peace, and joy in the Holy Spirit (Romans 14:17). The mindset of grace aims our thoughts in this direction. One of the core themes of this book is how we grow in grace. It's all about how the renewed mind operates in this new system of grace.

When the apostle Paul was converted on the road to Damascus, the attitude of his mind changed directions. His mind remained great, as always, for Paul was a brilliant man. What changed was the direction of his mind. His inward life had been transformed by God. He no longer adorned himself with righteousness based on good works. He even called his former way of life dung: "I count all things but loss for the excellency of the knowledge of Christ Jesus my Lord: for whom I have suffered the loss of all things and do count them but dung, that I may win Christ" (Philippians 3:8). Richard Rohr writes, "At this point, God becomes more a verb than a noun, more a process than a conclusion, more an experience than a dogma, more a personal relationship than an idea. There is someone dancing with you and you are not afraid of making mistakes."[88]

THE REWARDS OF THE NEW SYSTEM

Also in Greek mythology, there's another person, Jason, that made it past the island of sirens. Upon nearing the islands, Jason had his lute player, Orpheus, play music which was louder and more beautiful, drowning out the sirens' songs. As long as Orpheus played, anyone listening only heard his music. The sirens' songs were ignored because Jason and his men were captivated by the sweeter music of the lute player. Like the call of the sirens', the world lures to us and beckons us to come and expose our hearts and our desires to things that enslave us and destroy us in the end. But like the lute player's song, the paradigm of grace is stronger and more beautiful than anything the world offers.

It goes back to what I said about identity change, not behavior change. We move from a mere belief system, the way Paul did, to an actual inner experience.[89] We have new eyes to see and new ears to hear the sweeter music of the Savior. Call it a system if you will. But what has changed is the spirit of our minds. We are seeing differently, thinking differently, behaving differently inside this system of grace. Think of the prodigal son. He entered the system of grace—the ring, the robe, the fattened calf, the party, the welcome home—all the will of the father. I'm sure the prodigal enjoyed the will of his father—because it was perfect and pleasing.

Let me end where I started: What if we became our own choice architects? What if we designed and organized the context of our own choices between stimulus and response within the system of grace? There's a sweeter life waiting for us. It's more than safeguarding against sin, it's living from an authentic vision of Whose we are and making choices that match our identity within the system of grace.

REFLECTIONS

1. Now that we know we are new creations, how do we behave if the past is gone and the new is here?

2. What is your definition of grace?

3. If God were to leave a note of love for you, what would it say?

THE OBSERVER EFFECT

Your direction, not your intention, determines your destination!
—ANDY STANLEY

One night at dinner, a man who had spent many summers in Maine, fascinated his companions by telling of his experiences in a little town named Flagstaff. The town was slated for flooding to accommodate the creation of a vast lake, necessitating the construction of a dam. In the months before it was to be flooded, all improvements and repairs in the whole town were stopped. What was the use of painting a house if it was to be covered with water in six months? Why repair anything when the whole village was to be wiped out? Week by week, the whole town became more and more bedraggled and sadder and sadder in appearance. Then he added by way of explanation: "Where there is no faith in the future, there is no power in the present."[90] And without faith, we stop making choices to grow.

When life hits a dead end, we have a tendency to think nothing will change and adopt a fixed mindset. We have no vision for the future and we find ourselves stuck. Instead, we must believe the journey is taking us in a new direction. This is what it means to have a paradigm shift. We see new things with new eyes. What we all want to see and know is God's will. How can I know God's will for my life? This is the question that we ask between stimulus and response. How does God want me to respond? My choice between stimulus and response must come from a different place, other than my circumstances. If my eyes see only destruction, then I will be like the people of Flagstaff and adopt a fixed mindset and stop growing.

Between stimulus and response, we must stop and observe. To renew our mind, we must first become an observer. We step outside our ego. We see this in the children of Israel. They were stuck between a rock and a hard place. The Red Sea before them and the Egyptian army attacking from behind. Their enemy coming for them, to reclaim them. But God offered them a new paradigm. He set up the Red Sea encounter in a way that made the children of Israel observers. "Do not be afraid. Stand firm and you will see the deliverance the Lord will bring you today. The Egyptians you see today you will never see again. The Lord will fight for you; you need only to be still" (Exodus 14:14). Why was being an observer so important? The space between stimulus (the Egyptian army attacking from behind) and response (run or fight) offered a moment for observation. They observed God's will for them. So, what am I looking for? We all want God's will. Likewise, if we can discover God's will, then we will find the life we've always longed for.

Every paradigm shift includes an *observer effect*, which is the proven ability of observation to influence outcomes. Remember, expectations shape outcomes. Dr. Caroline Leaf, in her book *Switch on the Brain,* writes about the observer effect in quantum physics:

> "The observer determines the direction in which the possibilities may collapse. In the quantum universe, as we—the observers—affect phenomena, space, and time, we turn possibilities into realities. Mind changes matter . . . There is an endless array of possible choices you can make at any one moment in time, but it is you, with your ability to think, who directs the choice. So you collapse all the probabilities into one choice . . . "[91]

It's like a football quarterback going through his progressions until he finds (observes) the open receiver. God's will is the open receiver waving his hands for the ball.

OBSERVER EFFECT
The proven ability of observation to influence outcomes.

What did the children of Israel observe? The desert, the sea, the enemy—these were their alternatives. But there was another choice on the scene that day. The presence of God moved from the front of the children of Israel to the rear where the advancing army approached. God positioned Himself to fight for them and kept the Egyptians from advancing on the camp and destroying the children of Israel before they could cross the Red Sea (Exodus 14:19–20). They observed that God was committed to making them free. He would fight for them. Then all of their alternatives collapsed into one choice—move on with God. They observed, then they moved. As they walked away from the Red Sea, the dead Egyptians floating on the seashore was a reminder that the past was dead. It was now behind them. God's will was ahead of them.

So, whatever you do during our study together, keep moving. Don't go back to bondage! Don't run back, when with God you can walk through. Discover the sacred path through all dead ends. The safe passage of God's will. Paul talked about this in 1 Corinthians 10:13 (NIV): "No temptation has overtaken you except what is common to mankind. And God is faithful; he will not let you be tempted beyond what you can bear. But when you are tempted, he will also provide a way out so that you can endure it." Observe the way out. It's always there. We may have just failed to see it.

THE OBSERVATION OF A PARADIGM SHIFT

Now how does the observer effect help us understand God's will? There's only one choice that's pleasing and perfect—God's will. "Do not conform to the pattern of this world, but be transformed by the renewing of your mind. Then you will be able to test and approve what God's will is—his good, pleasing and perfect will" (Romans 12:2 NIV). God's will is the safe passage through the dark night of the soul. God's will is to see you free. This is the direction. This is the sacred path. Our journey to transformation is traveling through the bondage of the past to our freedom on the other side. This is a wonderful example of what happens between stimulus and response. We collapse all probabilities into one choice—God's will. The end result of a renewed mind is knowing the perfect and pleasing will of God.

The observer effect created a paradigm shift for the children of Israel because they were learning and growing as they watched. No longer were they obeying blindly as they had in Egypt, they were observing a place of love and trust—a direction away from their former bondage. They were learning to use their Reflective System that had never been used in slavery. This is what observation does for us. It creates a moment when our brains produce acetylcholine and it says "pay attention." Be still. Watch. Observe my ways. Then a direction opens up that takes us in the direction of God's will.

When they were at a dead end—trapped by a sea in front and an advancing army in the rear—there was still a possibility. They wanted to panic, but God wanted them to observe how a single probability could emerge—the dividing of the Red Sea. It's hard to imagine the scene. The howling wind and spray of foam, the earth trembling beneath their feet, the full paschal moon shining on the hardened sand, as Psalm 77 depicts it. I'm sure it was hard to move on, but they stepped into the sacred space—between walls of water and upon dry land. Sacred space can be terrifying before it becomes a safe passage requiring us to trust instead of reacting out of fear.

They never expected the way of escape until they observed it. How we see is what we see. To see rightly is to be able to be fully present—without fear, without bias, and without judgment[92] and without rebellion.

DISCOVERING GOD'S WILL FOR OUR LIVES

We always say that discovering God's will for our lives is a difficult thing. If God would just tell us, then we could act. Dr. D. Martyn Lloyd-Jones, once wrote regarding Romans 12:2, "The apostle, therefore, is telling us that those who renew their minds and obey the leading of the Spirit, will be able to discover certain things about the will of God. This is the most important thing that we can ever do and this is what the renewing of the mind as the result of our salvation enables us to do."[93]

God wants us to learn His ways. That's all He asks of us. "Know me," God says. "Observe My ways." Then you will know the direction to take.

He made known His ways to Moses,
His deeds to the people of Israel.

—PSALM 103:7

For forty years I was angry with that generation;
I said, "They are a people whose hearts go astray,
and they have not known my ways."

—PSALM 95:10

Here's my main idea for today: **God asks us to observe His ways before He gives us an action and then we act out of this observation.** "Picture the deliverance . . . picture the dead Egyptians." What a wonderful vision before anything had even occurred! "But God demonstrates his own love for us in this: While we were still sinners, Christ died for us" (Romans 5:8 NIV). God is always miles ahead of us, planning and working things out in advance. And the Israelite's abusers were all but dead. Soon they would catch a glimpse of the way

God would lead them into the future. God's will always points toward the growth mindset. We can achieve greater things by perceiving what is going on around us. What is God doing? Where is He leading? His will always leads us toward greater freedom.

The children of Israel were "baptized unto Moses" (1 Corinthians 10:2). They committed their direction to following Moses, just as Christian baptism shows a commitment to follow Christ. They chose his paradigm, his lens upon the world. They were united with him by trusting him. "And when the Israelites saw the mighty hand of the Lord displayed against the Egyptians, the people feared the Lord and put their trust in him and in Moses his servant" (Exodus 14:31). Trust is always the end result of observing God's ways. We trust His direction for our lives and discover His perfect and pleasing will. "Trust in the Lord with all your heart and lean not on your own understanding; in all your ways submit to Him and He will make your paths straight" (Proverbs 3:5-6). God's will is a direction.

FAITH OR DOUBT

Picture deliverance first, not fear first. The dead Egyptians on the seashore made them realize that their oppression was over, their chains eternally broken. They were introduced into a new life, which was free will, a basic ingredient of quantum physics. Directing our attention to God's will sends us in the direction of happiness. On the other side of the Red Sea, Moses' sister, Miriam, sang her song with timbrel in hand, while all the women followed suit, "Sing to the LORD, for he is highly exalted. Both horse and driver he has hurled into the sea" (Exodus 15:21). They aligned their minds with God's will and their body and soul danced. They praised.

We can respond in faith or in doubt. Deep transformation happens when we observe and make choices from the sacred space where the Divine dwells. It's where we observe how loved we truly are, for we cannot move against fear without love. This is why John wrote, "There is no fear in love. But perfect love drives out fear, because fear has to do with punishment. The one who fears is not made perfect in love" (1 John 4:18).

One of the best examples of grace I've ever heard—outside the Bible—came from Paul Harvey. In Paul Harvey's, *For What It's Worth*:

> "Carl Coleman was driving to work, according to Quote magazine, when a woman motorist, passing too close, snagged his fender with hers.
>
> Both cars stopped.
>
> The young woman surveying the damage was in tears.
>
> It was her fault, she admitted.
>
> But it was a new car—less than two days from the showroom.
>
> How was she ever going to face her husband?
>
> Mr. Coleman was sympathetic but explained they must note each other's license number and registration.
>
> She reached into the glove compartment to retrieve the documents in an envelope . . .
>
> And on the first paper to tumble out, in a heavy masculine scrawl, were these words:
>
> "In case of accident, remember, Honey, it's you I love, not the car."[94]

What a paradigm shift! In a sense, the husband was saying, "Nothing can separate you from my love." What a great picture of what unconditional love is.

Love is greater than any habit. It's the lens of the new paradigm—in Christ. We are loved and secure. If we can open our eyes to this kind of love, then we grow. The chains of guilt and condemnation fall off.

Let the divine inside your soul. This sacred center will become the command post for all your actions. Everything must travel through this sacred space where we observe His deliverance. "Keep yourselves in the love of God, looking for the mercy of our Lord Jesus Christ unto eternal life" (Jude 1:21). It changes the patterns of this world by collapsing the probabilities into a choice in the direction of our Lord. We walk by faith in the context of the kingdom of God, not by sight in this world. So, let's take a moment today and begin to observe.

REFLECTIONS:

1. What are you observing about God's activity in your life? Do you feel His presence?

2. Can you describe a moment in your past when you felt God was guiding you toward His will?

3. Can you think of a situation in your past where you could have
   paused between stimulus and response?

WHAT'S REALLY GOING ON HERE?

*Usually, the first problems you solve with the new paradigm are
the ones that were unsolvable with the old paradigm.*

—JOEL A. BARKER

On July 6, 1994, nine members of a highly trained hotshot crew, along with five other wildland firefighters and smokejumpers lost their lives in a wildfire on Storm King Mountain in Colorado. The hotshot crew from Prineville, Oregon was sent in to fight the most challenging parts of the fire. That afternoon a dry cold front passed through the area and increased the winds, which further ignited the fire. By 4 p.m., the fire had spotted beyond the fire line and below the firefighter's location to the west and chased them up the steep, densely vegetated terrain.

Four women and ten men ran for their lives loaded down with all of their equipment—axes, saws, shovels, and 20-pound packs. All fourteen were just 200 feet from safety when the fire overtook them. How could this happen to highly trained firefighters? What decisions led to this tragedy? There were others fighting the fire on the mountain that day that survived. So how did some of the firefighters survive and others die?

For a hotshot crew to effectively perform their duties, hotshot crews must be able to correlate with the time it takes to reach a safety zone. They must maintain a high level of physical fitness. Aerobic fitness is correlated with the time it takes to reach a safety zone. The minimum physical fitness standards for hotshots set by the National Wildfire Coordinating Group are: a 3-mile hike carrying a 60-pound pack under 90 minutes, one and a half-mile run in 10:30 or less, 25 push-ups in 60 seconds, 45 sit-ups in 60 seconds and 7 pull-ups. These are the bare minimum requirements prescribed by policy and most hotshots far exceed these requirements.[95] So how did these firefighters get it so wrong? There has been much debate over the years about policy failure and poor decision-making on their part. Later investigators calculated that without their tools and backpacks, the crew would have moved 15 to 20% faster. "Most would have lived had they simply dropped their gear and run for safety," one expert wrote. The U.S. Forestry Service agreed. If they had "dropped their packs and tools, the firefighters would have reached the top of the ridge before the fire."[96]

Why did this not occur to them?

Maybe it had something to do with their training. They were trained to outrun a fire with all of their gear. Or maybe it had something to do with their identity as firefighters. Is this it? Were they overconfident? It happens. Their calculations were off by 15 to 20%. Enough to cost them their lives. If they had only dropped their gear. Just maybe they would be alive today.

Why did the firefighters continue to carry tools they no longer needed? Organizational psychologist Karl Weick, commenting on the fire, writes, "Fires are not fought with bodies and bare hands, they are fought with tools that are often distinctive trademarks of firefighters. They are the firefighter's reason for being deployed in the first place . . . Dropping one's tools creates an existential crisis. Without my tools, who am I?"[97]

In a YouTube video, one of the survivors of the fire said, "My chainsaw had a name and it was my tool and I cared for it a lot. I never thought about putting it down. But eventually I saw a stack of chainsaws and I dropped mine there."[98] The surprise of seeing that those ahead of him had dropped their gear nudged him into dropping his own chainsaw.

Gary Klein, in his book, *Seeing What Others Don't: The Remarkable Ways We Gain Insights,* writes about firefighters, "The most dramatic scenarios, however, contained surprises that forced the firefighters to rethink what was going on and replace erroneous beliefs." That pile of chainsaws surprised him and replaced his erroneous belief that carrying his tools was still safe. Without surprise, our erroneous beliefs never change.

The reason we don't create the life we've always wanted is because we have a hard time throwing things off and throwing them out. Anyone who has cleaned out their garage knows what I mean. We think, "I might need this one day." But it goes a step deeper when the item we are being asked to throw out has sentimental value/may have had purpose in our lives, like the chainsaw the firefighter had named.

Richard Rohr believes we ask one of two questions when facing adversity: 1) How does my self-image demand that I react to this? 2) How can I get back in control of this situation?[99] When these two questions rule our thoughts, we usually revert back to our erroneous beliefs to save face and to protect the ego.

Maybe a crisis brought you to this book. Maybe you were nudged by adversity to seek change. You are ahead of the curve. Research has proven that under acute stress, people typically revert to their automatic, well-learned responses.[100] In moments of stress when change is possible, we revert, instead of change. We fall back to our default systems. It seems the explorer Hernán Cortez knew this. Upon arriving in the "new world," he ordered his men to burn the ships. No retreat seems to be the lesson, but maybe it did more than that. Maybe it reset their default systems. If your default system is to retreat to the ships under an acute attack or because the new land is strange and uncomfortable, then what happens if you take the ships away? You've eliminated a default setting. You've changed the rules of engagement. No retreats. You have to stay and fight.

RUNNING ON AUTOPILOT

Our transformation requires a factory settings change beneath the hood of our automatic system. David Eagleman says our conscious mind works like the CEO of a large sprawling corporation, with many thousands of subdivisions and departments all collaborating and interacting and competing in different ways. He says consciousness gets involved when the unexpected happens, when we need to work out what to do next. He writes, "But consciousness isn't just about reacting to surprises. It also plays a vital role in settling conflict within the brain."[101] To change our autopilots, we must get the Reflective System involved, which occurs when we are surprised and must ask, "What's going on here?"

The firefighters on Storm King Mountain had trained for emergencies. Their muscle memory told them they could outrun the fire. Over the years they had established a default system on emergency situations. And once this default system took over, it was difficult to reason with their prefrontal cortexes. It took the surprise of a pile of chainsaws to nudge the one who had named his chainsaw to drop it on the pile. It wasn't what he expected to see and this surprise changed the logic in his automatic system. That pile of chainsaws was a powerful nudge of surprise: "What's really going on here?" Nudges of surprise stop our unconscious autopilots and create moments of self-awareness.

THE NUDGE OF SURPRISE

Tania Luna, the co-author of the book, *Surprise: Embrace the Unpredictable and Engineer the Unexpected,* writes: "(Surprise) is a strong neuro alert that tells us that something is important about this moment and we have to pay attention. Our cognitive resources are basically hijacked and pulled into the moment. That's one of the things that's really uncomfortable for some people, but also exciting for some people because your attention is completely in the moment."[102] This is what happened to the firefighter and the pile of chainsaws. It pulled him into the moment in a new way. It made him pay attention. He asked, "What's really going on here?" And he realized the need to lighten his load.

Luna writes, "When we're surprised, for better or for worse, our emotions intensify up to 400%."[103] That's an intense spike. Luna says that being surprised actually causes humans to physically freeze for 1/25th of a second. It generates extreme curiosity in an attempt to figure out what is happening during a surprise. We stop and ask, "What's really going on here?" Surprise causes us to hunt for underlying causes, to imagine other possibilities, to figure out how to avoid surprises in the future.[104]

Think of Moses and the burning bush. "Moses thought, 'I will go over and see this strange sight—why the bush does not burn up'" (Exodus 3:3). It was a strange sight that surprised him and piqued his curiosity because it usually took a desert bush seconds to burn up, but this one strangely kept burning. So Moses asked, "What's going on here?" And through this gate of curiosity, Moses discovered the very heart of God's presence in the burning bush.

Chuck Swindoll writes, "God may use an extraordinary event or circumstance to tap you on the shoulder, in order to grab your attention. He may use something like that to intrude into your daily life and say, 'Wait a minute. Stop. Be still. I have something to say to you.' When you and I come across extremely unusual events, it's a good idea to ask: 'Could God be saying something to me now?'"[105] This is what I want you to continually ask yourself, as you move through our time together.

We get stuck in a toxic life when we stop looking for new insights and fail to stop and ask, "What's really going on here?" It creates openings for making new discoveries and new insights. We are no longer helpless and hopeless. We experience the observer effect.

After surprise piques our curiosity, Luna says surprise offers a paradigm shift. She says, "If the surprise is something that forces you to change your perspective, then you have to change the way you've been looking at things. If I wasn't expecting you to surprise me or give me a gift and now I've just gotten this pleasant experience, I have to change the way I think about you and maybe even our whole relationship."[106]

Why did God speak to Moses through a burning bush? It created curiosity and a paradigm shift. This surprise brought his conscious mind online and helped to recommission him, creating the life he had always wanted. He had always wanted to be Israel's deliverer, but he had given up on it after he killed an Egyptian and fled to the desert for forty years. Now at the age of 80, God's surprise changed everything. That morning he was a murderer and a shepherd. After the burning bush encounter, he was a leader and builder of a nation. It changed the way he viewed himself and the world. It was a huge paradigm shift. Everything changed for Moses after this encounter. Suddenly, he understood God's perfect will for his life.

Remain open as we move through this study. God's messages are everywhere if we are curious enough to look. Jesus said in Luke 12:24-28: "Consider the ravens: They do not sow or reap, they have no storeroom or barn; yet God feeds them. And how much more valuable you are than birds! Who of you by worrying can add a single hour to your life? Since you cannot do this very little thing, why do you worry about the rest?"

God's Post-it notes are evocative and pervasive throughout nature. The sea wants to speak to us, but we don't listen to its voice. The stars are calling out to us, but we hardly ever look up with wonder and curiosity. Start looking for God's Post-it notes by looking up. Looking up fires dopamine and opens the realm of possibility, so ask God to surprise you.

Get some Post-it notes and begin to look around for surprises, then jot them down on the Post-it notes or journal about them. Start looking for new possibilities. See what happens. You will be surprised. Moses allowed nature and God to surprise him. He got curious and it changed the direction of his life—at the age of 80, he asked, "What's going on here?" So did the children of Israel.

And to add to this, I think of the story of Jacob dreaming of a stairway to heaven. "When Jacob awoke from his sleep, he thought, 'Surely the

Lord is in this place and I was not aware of it'" (Genesis 28:16). This is the great psychological and spiritual discovery that only happens once we stop conforming to the patterns of this world and ask, "What's really going on here?"

REFLECTIONS

1. When surprised by adversity, such as a health issue, a job layoff, a broken relationship, or a debt crisis, how do you respond? Do you revert to thinking old negative thoughts or do you pause, get curious and look for new answers?

2. Throughout this week, look for surprises and journal or write down in this space the surprises you encounter.

HABITS NEED MORE THAN FRICTION

Bad habits are like comfortable beds—
easy to get into but hard to get out of.

—ANONYMOUS

An elderly teacher, with a pupil by his side, took a walk through a forest. Suddenly he stopped and pointed to four plants close at hand. The first was just beginning to peep above the ground, the second had rooted itself pretty well into the earth, the third was a small shrub, while the fourth was a full-sized tree. The tutor said to his young companion, "Pull up the first plant." The boy did so eagerly, using only his fingers.

"Now pull up the second." The youth obeyed but found the task more difficult.

"Do the same with the third," he urged. The boy had to use all his strength to uproot it.

"Now," said the instructor, "try your hand with the fourth." The pupil put his arms around the trunk of the tall tree and couldn't even shake its leaves.

"This, my son, is just what happens with our bad habits. When they are young, we can remove them readily; but when they are old, it's hard to uproot them, though we pray and struggle ever so sincerely."[107]

Habits are difficult to change because they are rooted in an old habit memory system. The brain has created this neural pathway and asks: "What have I done in the past that has gotten a reward?" The habit system focuses on past rewards.[108] And some habits are like that tree. For good habits, this is a good thing. For bad habits, we have to work a little harder to free ourselves, but it can be done.

One of the things we can do to break an easy habit is change our mindset toward the habit by adding what behavioral scientists call— adding friction. **When the brain has to work harder to perform a habit, it loses interest.** We can make a habit harder to perform.[109] Take this example of adding friction from cigarette smoking. Smoking bans in English pubs made it more difficult for people with strong smoking habits to light up while drinking. Having to leave the pub adds friction.[110] Ulysses added friction and made it harder to respond to the sirens' song. But who wants to tie themselves to the mast and live under the constant threat of temptation? There's a better way.

Changing the attitude of my mind toward that habit is how we put on the new self. I continue to grow, not impede growth, which is what I believe adding friction does. It comes from a fixed mindset. It attempts to block the habit by making it harder to perform, in hopes that the brain will get disinterested and say, "I'm not doing it anymore. It's too hard." This in many ways is reformation, not transformation.

Reformation is just swapping to a new habit that's easier. Transformation is the new self with a renewed mind that desires a deeper sense of God. Reformation can work and does work with a lot of effort. Ask Ulysses. It can save our lives, so I'm not against reformation. But if God's will is His commitment to our freedom, then I think it's far superior to observe and collapse our choice in the direction of His transforming grace. How does it work?

Let's take a look at Ephesians 4:22-24 (NIV) to see how our attitude can change a habit: "You were taught, with regard to your former way of life, to put off your old self, which is being corrupted by its deceitful desires; to be made new in the attitude of your minds; and to put on the new self, created to be like God in true righteousness and holiness."

The key phrase is: made new in the attitude of your minds. Can we change the attitude of our minds toward our deceitful desires? Gerald May puts it like this:

> "Through grace, with our assent, our desire begins to be transformed. Energies that were once dedicated simply to relieving ourselves from pain now become dedicated to a larger goodness, more aligned with the true treasure of our hearts. Where we were once interested only in conquering a specific addiction, we are now claiming a deeper longing and we are concerned with becoming more free from attachments in general, for the sake of love. What had begun as an expedient attempt to reform a behavior has now become a process of transforming a life."[111]

Going in the direction of God's will consecrates our struggles—makes them sacred. Uprooting bad habits tills up the soil of freedom so new desires can grow. We are no longer hacking at the leaves but striking at the root. It occurs when our observation of God's commitment to make us free becomes our choice for His direction toward this freedom. This is putting on the new self (Ephesians 4:24). God puts something in us that was not there before—His love and the desire to make us free. It is not just an improvement of the old self. It's being a new creation. This is what it means to be a Christian. We are not trying to reform behavior but transform at the center where we participate with the Divine (theosis). We see this in 2 Peter 1:4: "Through these he has given us his very great and precious promises, so that through them you may participate in the divine nature, having escaped the corruption in the world caused by evil desires." It changes the attitude of our minds because our minds are participating with the Divine. We're choosing and responding from this center of the Divine within. Now we have a new mindset for all our choices and a desire to please Him. It's more than just making it harder to perform the bad habit. I'm choosing from a new place of unconditional love.

THEOSIS
A transformative process in which the aim is likeness to or union with God.

Don't get me wrong, it will take a deliberate action to move in the direction of God's perfect and pleasing will. For the children of Israel to move out of their bondage, they had to travel through a safe passage. The old was left behind, the new was received. They became a holy nation, a greater version, the one God kept insisting they already were. Habit change is a matter of the heart. I cocreate a new attitude toward the old habit. It's more than adding friction. I move in a new direction entirely. I consecrate my desires.

DAVID AND HIS BOYHOOD DESIRE

Hiding out from his enemy in the sweltering heat of a cave, King David remembered the days of his youth and longed for a drink from the well at Bethlehem, where he once watered his flocks (2 Samuel 23:15). He said, "Oh, that someone would get me a drink of water from the well near the gate of Bethlehem!" It wasn't a direct command, but three of his mighty warriors overheard this longing and planned a surprise for David. They broke through the ranks of the Philistine army and traveled to the well and brought back the water David had longed for. But David wasn't pleased with the water, for it seemed to be dyed with the blood of his men. It had become too precious to be used to satisfy his longing, so he poured it out as a drink offering to the Lord.

Today, we would call it buyer's remorse. We may want a new sports car but suffer buyer's remorse when we don't like the high payments each month. Wanting and liking come from two different systems in the brain.[112] The *Here* and *Now* (H&N) molecules are serotonin, oxytocin, endorphins (your brain's version of morphine), and a class of chemicals called endocannabinoids (your brain's version of marijuana). These chemicals give us pleasure from sensation and emotion and make us feel satisfied.

HERE & NOW CHEMICALS (H&N'S)
Chemicals in our brain that allow you to experience satisfaction and enjoy whatever you feel in the here and now.

Then there's another chemical in the brain called dopamine that gives us the pleasure of anticipation.[113] Rewards are dopaminergic because dopamine is the salesperson that tells us how happy we will be to obtain this or that. This is the battle of habits. This is why habits are hard to change.

When dopamine promises to fulfill our longing, to quench our thirst, (whatever the neurological craving may be), it doesn't often think about the response of the H&N's, which are the chemicals in the brain that make us feel satisfied. This is why we don't always like the things we want, i.e., buyer's remorse. We may want a new car but hate the payments once we buy it. And, usually, our brain likes the rewards that it wants. But sometimes it may just want them.[114] And it doesn't have a real plan about how to like them on a long-term basis. This becomes a bad habit. We want, but we don't like. Liking something on a long-term basis comes from a sense of satisfaction. What offers us this state of mind are the H&Ns. But I'll focus on one of the H&Ns that has been overlooked until recently—oxytocin.

Studies have shown that oxytocin gives the brain an extended release of satisfaction. Learning how to link the H&Ns with dopamine in the brain is the key to transformation and long-term satisfaction. Paul J. Zak, who first studied the release of oxytocin in the brain, calls it the moral molecule. He writes in the *Harvard Business Review*,

"Experiments show that having a sense of higher purpose stimulates oxytocin production, as does trust. Trust and purpose then mutually reinforce each other, providing a mechanism for extended oxytocin release, which produces happiness."[115]

Dopamine plays no role in generating feelings of satisfaction. It just wants. The thrill of obtaining what we desire—such as drugs, gambling, and other out-of-control behaviors—can destroy our lives. [116]

But why can't the H&Ns reel in dopamine? Our wants must match our likes. But why is it so hard to link the two together? Most attachments, as well as stress, inhibits the release of the H&Ns, because in the end, bad habits don't satisfy. They take us in the direction of guilt and condemnation. This is the fixed mindset of buyer's remorse, which is the backside of dopamine.

THE ROLE OF OXYTOCIN

Oxytocin is a powerful surge of happiness in the brain. This is why our brains enjoy having a higher purpose and a sense of trust. So bridging dopamine and the H&Ns (Oxytocin) is a matter of having a higher purpose and trusting God with our future. David does this with the water his mighty warriors gave him. The Bible says he refused to drink it. Instead, he poured it out before the Lord. "Far be it from me, Lord, to do this!" he said. "Is it not the blood of men who went at the risk of their lives? And David would not drink it" (2 Samuel 23:16-17).

Between stimulus and response, David gave this dopaminergic wish for water from the well near Bethlehem a higher purpose by pouring it out as a libation or drink offering, to the Lord. It was a solemn consecration of this dangerously won water. The attitude of his mind toward this dopamine wish changed when he felt the empathy of his men towards him. He sensed their love and sacrifice and this changed his desire. There are three types of empathy that produce oxytocin:

1. **Cognitive Empathy:** the ability to understand another's perspective. We think about their feelings rather than feel them directly.

2. **Emotional Empathy:** the ability to physically feel what another person feels. This type of empathy helps people feel attuned to another person's emotions and provides the ability to feel others' emotions quickly without thinking deeply.

3. **Empathic Concern:** the ability to sense what someone needs from you.[117]

Why is empathy so important to changing habits? Empathy creates grace which pulls us towards change which creates intrinsic motivation. Because oxytocin activates a brain network that makes us more empathic.[118] And what activates oxytocin is a sense of higher purpose and trust. "Many are the woes of the wicked, but the LORD's unfailing love surrounds the one who trusts in him" (Psalm 32:10). When I sense God's love, I'm understanding and sharing feelings with Him. This satisfies my soul. It's also interesting that studies have shown that those who believe in a judgmental and punitive God, produce more testosterone, which is an oxytocin inhibitor. Testosterone nudges us toward fear and punishment. But if we believe God is the God of love, then we release oxytocin and oxytocin nudges our behavior toward love and connection.[119] Bad habits nudge us toward guilt and condemnation.

Our paradigm of God matters. Between stimulus and response, we must choose a God of love and the release of oxytocin will nudge our behavior in the direction of connecting with God's will.

As Stephen Covey puts it, "I can tie myself to my limitless potential instead of my limiting past . . . so that the paradigms from which my behavior and attitude flow are congruent with my deepest values and in harmony with correct principles."[120]

David was able to do this. He tied the moment to a limitless potential (consecration) and from this paradigm he envisioned a higher purpose for the water, raising his H&N levels. He valued his men and gave the water a higher meaning. His response satisfied his soul and produced harmony.

Gerald May writes, "Ultimately, our yearning for God is the most important aspect of our humanity, our most precious treasure; it gives our existence meaning and direction." Remember, this is what the observer effect did for the children of Israel. They found meaning in God's commitment to free them and moved in that direction. **If our wants aren't taking us in the direction of God's will, then we will never be satisfied.** You'll remain in buyer's remorse—the mindset of guilt and condemnation. Unbridled dopamine will wreck your life.

We must ask ourselves in the space between stimulus and response: "What will satisfy my soul?" Soul-satisfaction is the link that connects dopamine and the H&Ns. It brings body, soul, and mind into balance. David created a soul-satisfying moment. He visualized his best self— his true self—and acted in accordance with his deepest held values. His final action matched the value of his changeless core.

When we see ourselves and our world through a different lens, a different narrative—participating with the Divine (theosis)—then we accept our higher purpose. Then the God-given oxytocin flows and we feel satisfaction in life. No longer suffering buyer's remorse (guilt and condemnation) from an out-of-control dopamine rush.

REFLECTIONS

1. What do you really want out of life?

2. Do you believe your life has a higher purpose?

3. Think of one bad habit—something that doesn't align with your values. Find the deeper longing behind it. Change your mindset toward the habit. Commit to only doing what satisfies your soul.

4. Now work to create a new habit in its place. The resulting satisfaction will give you an oxytocin rush. Line up your new behavior with your highest values.

THE GREAT AND PRECIOUS PROMISES OF GOD

Our true identity is to love without fear and insecurity.
Our higher potential finds us when we set our course in that direction.
The power of love and compassion transforms insecurity.

—DOC CHILDRE

Wendy Wood conducted a study with movie theater popcorn to back up her findings about habits. Researchers gave people about to enter a movie theater a bucket of either just-popped fresh popcorn, or stale week-old popcorn. Moviegoers who didn't usually eat popcorn at the movies ate much less stale popcorn than fresh popcorn. The week-old popcorn just didn't taste as good.

But moviegoers who indicated that they typically had popcorn at the movies ate about the same amount of popcorn whether it was fresh or stale. In other words, for those in the habit of having popcorn at the movies, it made no difference whether the popcorn tasted good or not.

This is their conclusion: "When we've repeatedly eaten a particular food in a particular environment, our brain comes to associate the food with that environment and make us keep eating as long as those environmental cues are present," said lead author David Neal, who was a psychology professor at USC when the research was conducted.[121]

The findings are you can't change habits by changing rewards. You must change the cues that activate behavior. The stable environment in this study is the movie theater. It is the cue. And our brain is wired to connect the behavior to the context (place), so we don't have to think in the future. It needs a placeholder outside of the brain that triggers the behavior. And for popcorn consumption, it's a movie theater. This is how conformity works. So, how do we transform a habit? We change the context.

Habits begin in the fertile soil of our environment. Think of most habits you've formed. They started in a place and time. The action cue is more likely to be located in a context such as "when watching television" or "in the evening as soon as we return home from work" or for coffee drinkers, "waking in the morning." As soil is for the tree, context is for habit formation. The environment triggers the craving. Behavioral scientists have long known that changing the performance environment changes our habits.

HABIT FORMATION REDUX

Let's go back over habit formation, but let's take a different lens. Wendy Wood gives us three key principles in forming a habit.[122] The first key is repetition. We repeat a behavior, such as going to the gym, on a regular basis to improve fitness. The second key is rewards, as we have seen. We repeat what gets rewarded, so the activity must be enjoyable. Make behavior fun. The third key is context, as we've seen above. Our performance context (what surrounds us when we do something) must be a stable context (stress-free).

Why is a stable context important? It's important because stress inhibits oxytocin. So, it makes sense that it must be a stress-free context cue. But it's hard to find places in this world without stress. These days life is stressful, but experts say we must have a stable context to create a habit. We must find a place of peace, then establish a new habit in this performance context.

But I think this is all backwards from the way we should form a new habit. For Christians, new habits must emerge from the new self. The context (place) that produces cues is from within. Changing from an outward cue to an inward cue takes us out of the fixed mindset of guilt and condemnation. Remember that transformation is something that takes place inside of us. Conformity takes place outside of us. We no longer conform to the patterns of this world, but transform by the renewing of our minds (Romans 12:2). To transform the behavior, we transform the context. We move from outward cues to inner cues.

Once we make this switch, our choices between stimulus and response are coming from the sacred center of our soul. The new cues emerge from the participation with the Divine. Think of how Jason changed the cue. He replaced the sirens' song with a magic lute player. It wasn't about more or less willpower. It was about something sweeter than the siren's song. It's the idea of hope. It's belief and expectancy.

Adding friction to our habits, as we've seen, just makes life more difficult. Changing the cue, changes the mindset. We need a new cue that comes from a new mindset. The magical lute player changed Jason's mindset. It's more than constricting our environment. We are transforming our environment by moving away from making choices based on outward circumstances.

God's grace should always be our main cue within, leading us toward better choices. Our habits must become kingdom habits. It proclaims what God has done for us now that the kingdom of God has arrived through Christ. Grace is where God begins with us. By nature, we cannot make ourselves righteous. Our righteousness is like filthy rags (Isaiah 64:6). "All of us have sinned and fallen short of God's glory" (Romans 3:23). Every thought should be rooted in grace and the love of God. If I'm choosing my behavior from this mindset, then I'm growing in love toward God and others. I'm hearing a sweeter song. Oxytocin is flowing. My wants are matching my likes. My present state of mind is matching my future self. We match our behavior to our goals. We do this by and through the great and precious promises of God.

THE GREAT AND PRECIOUS PROMISES OF GOD

Let's take another look at 2 Peter 1:4: "Through these he has given us his very great and precious promises, so that through them you may participate in the divine nature, having escaped the corruption in the world caused by evil desires." God's promises are the sweeter music. Through God's promises, we participate with the divine nature. When our mind rehearses God's promises, it lives in the presence of God and we escape the corruption that is in the world. We open our minds to the unseen. We hear a sweeter music. We partake of the divine nature. We are not just forgiven in Christ but are partakers of the divine nature. We see with the mind of Christ. This is the great paradigm shift of the faith. Christ becomes the paradigm.

We dwell in the center where the great and precious promises have already been given. Think of it as a storehouse. We take what we need when we need it. We are not subject to the cues of the world. We are in the world, but not of it. When we need something, we go to God first. We look around the kingdom at His promises, then take the one we need to cue behavior.

For example, if I feel anxious and want what I want now, then I can cue a different thought by reading one of God's promises, such as: "For still the vision awaits its appointed time; it hastens to the end—it will not lie. If it seems slow, wait for it; it will surely come; it will not delay" (Habakkuk 2:3). Here's another: "Let us not become weary in doing good, for at the proper time we will reap a harvest if we do not give up" (Galatians 6:9).

These are not just words. They are promises. And everything we say and do must come from participating with the divine nature by accepting His timetable and by trusting that the harvest is on its way. See how this cue overcomes thoughts of despair? If we accept His promise and keep doing good, then we won't grow weary. Our present self is moving in God's direction and connecting with our future self. We walk by faith and not by sight. We see into the unseen world.

No matter the circumstances of your life, practice being present to Christ. The key is to have an integrated life with integrated actions, integrated choices, and integrated thoughts. Whatever you feed your soul, your mind, and your heart will determine your outcome. Inputs determine outputs. You're either going to grow new neural pathways or old neural pathways will remain. You can't be afraid of your past. You can't allow your past to hold you hostage. You can't stay stuck in the past and feel sorry for yourself, regretting what you failed to accomplish. You've got to let go of all of it. Making room (kenosis) by emptying out the world and our attachments, then the Divine comes in (theosis) and we are deeply transformed.

REFLECTIONS

1. Choose a problem you are facing right now in your life. Now search through the thousands of promises in the Bible to match what you need. Meditate on this Scripture today. Then choose a different one tomorrow.

2. Share with the group how this process has helped you overcome a problem?

BREAK THE HABIT OF
BEING YOURSELF

HOW TO SILENCE THE INNER CRITIC

Success isn't measured by money or power or social rank.
Success is measured by your discipline and inner peace.

—MIKE DITKA

Ever heard of the "Florida Effect?" I'm not talking about politics or moving to Florida. The "Florida Effect" is a study about how your actions and your emotions can be primed by events you are not aware of. It works like this. In an experiment that became an instant classic, the psychologist John Bargh asked students at New York University—most aged eighteen to twenty-two—to assemble four-word sentences from a set of five words. For example, "finds he it yellow instantly," which could be unscrambled as, "Instantly, he finds yellow." For one group of students, half the scrambled sentences contained words associated with the elderly, such as Florida, forgetful, bald, gray, or wrinkle.

FLORIDA OR IDEOMOTOR EFFECT
Powerful example of "priming" which is the use of background factors to put someone in a psychological state that affects their actions without their conscious knowledge.

When they had completed the task, the young participants were sent out to do another experiment in an office down the hall. That short walk was what the experiment was about. The researchers unobtrusively measured the time it took people to get from one end of the corridor to the other. As Bargh had predicted, the young people who had fashioned a sentence from words with an elderly theme walked down the hallway significantly more slowly than the others.

That is the "Florida Effect." Daniel Kahneman says "The "Florida Effect" involves two stages of priming. First, the set of words primes thoughts of old age, though the word "old" is never mentioned; second, these thoughts prime a behavior, walking slowly, which is associated with old age. All this happens without any awareness."[123]

The students never noticed that the words had a common theme and they didn't believe these words had influenced them. The idea of old age had not come to their conscious awareness.

Let's do our own experiment. I'll give you two words. One of the words will have one letter missing, so your participation is to finish the word by interjecting the letter to complete the word.

WASH
SO_P

EAT
SO_P

In psychology proper this is known as the *ideomotor effect*— the influencing of an action by the idea. WASH primes the idea of SOAP. And EAT primes the idea of SOUP. It's always amazing when science research catches up with ancient Scripture. Paul writes in 2 Corinthians 10:4-5: "The weapons we fight with are not the weapons of the world. On the contrary, they have divine power to demolish strongholds. We demolish arguments and every pretension that sets itself up against the knowledge of God and we take captive every thought to make it obedient to Christ."

Paul knew about the "Florida Effect" or the ideomotor effect, even though he didn't name it. He knew our thoughts influence our behavior, so he said we must take captive every thought.

We live in a world where we are being primed by messages every minute of the day to buy something, use something, believe in something, doubt something, argue against something. Never have we been so bombarded with messages and most of these messages influence us in ways that are unconscious. This is the danger. We are being influenced to act by the idea being planted in our brains—the ideomotor effect. For this reason, Paul tells us to "take our thoughts captive." He believes in the ideomotor effect. He knows the danger of a toxic Automatic System running on autopilot.

THE INNER CRITIC

As we've learned, our habits can run beneath our conscious awareness and the most toxic element in the Automatic System is the *inner critic*. It takes up residence at the center of our soul intended for the Spirit of God. The inner critic reminds us of our frailty and faults. Like the "Florida Effect," it plants ideas in our mind of inferiority. We believe others perceive us as failures because we perceive ourselves as failures. We personify the inner critic, making it the spokesperson for the way the world sees us. It nags and deceives. No matter how we perform, it likes to tell us what we "should" have done, not allowing us to enjoy any success. It makes us feel deeply inadequate. But taking our thoughts captive will demolish the stranglehold of the inner critic.

Most of the time the inner critic is running unobserved and unhindered in our Automatic System. We've gotten used to its thoughts and influence and to silence it, we must stop the autopilot of our unconscious thoughts. This is what "taking our thoughts captive" can do for us. Remember, to change the Automatic System, the Reflective System must get involved. We stop letting it run in our unconscious mind unhindered. We must pay attention to the pattern of our thoughts and rethink the validity of the inner critic's assault. It's not easy, but it can be done.

We change the way we are thinking by thinking Christ's thoughts. This is the knowledge that doesn't exalt itself above the knowledge of God (2 Corinthians 10:5). The inner critic cannot exist where Christ dwells. No matter the circumstances of your life, practice being present to Christ.

The key is to have an integrated life—inner and outer worlds aligning—with integrated actions, integrated choices, and integrated thoughts. Whatever you feed your soul, your mind and your heart will determine your outcome. **Expectations shape outcomes.** You're either going to grow new neural pathways or old neural pathways will remain.

How can I silence the inner critic? I must take captive its thoughts and replace these thoughts with the voice of God, which will prune negative thoughts and eliminate the inner critic. It sets a new default setting in our minds. This is how powerful thoughts can be when we use them. Our inner world has to be greater than the outer world, or we will be victims of our environment. So, I must take some action that will interrupt the inner critic. Then make the ideomotor effect work for us. How? You must prime your thoughts with new thoughts. When the inner critic harasses you, then prime a new thought by using one of God's promises, which is how we participate with the divine nature (2 Peter 1:4). For example, use this verse from Romans 8:31 to prime new thoughts: "If God is for us, who can be against us?" It goes back to having an if-then plan. If the inner critic says this, then I'll say that.

Remember what Dr. Joe Dispenza said: "So if we want to change some aspect of our reality, we have to think, feel, and act in new ways; we have to 'be' different in terms of our responses to experiences. We have to 'become' someone else. We have to create a new state of mind . . . we need to observe a new outcome with that new mind."[124] This is how you put off the old self and put on the new self (Ephesians 4:22). We prime new thoughts that lead to the new self. Think of the oyster. It takes a grain of sand and turns it into a beautiful pearl. Too often we are just the opposite—we take pearls and turn them into a grain of sand. Has something been your past? Don't let it be your future! Start priming your thoughts for a new outcome.

REFLECTIONS

1. Do you have an inner critic?

2. How are your thoughts priming your behavior?

3. What are some ways to think positive thoughts, instead of negative ones?

AIMING OUR THOUGHTS HIGHER

It is storied of Henry the Fourth of France,
asking the Duke of Alva if he had observed the eclipses
happening in that year, he answered, that he had so much
business on earth, that he had no leisure to look up to heaven.

—J. SPENCE

There's an amusing, but informative architectural design in the men's rooms at Schiphol Airport in Amsterdam. In the men's urinal, authorities etched the image of a black housefly. It seems that men do not pay much attention to where they aim. But if they see a target, their attention and accuracy get much better. Aad Kieboom, an economist, who directed Schiphol's building expansion, came up with the idea. He said, "It improves the aim. If a man sees a fly, he aims at it." His staff conducted experiments that discovered the etchings of black houseflies in urinals reduced spillage by 80%.[125] In a men's urinal, aim is a good thing.

In the last chapter, we discussed how the Automatic System must be interrupted by capturing our thoughts and redirecting them. We do this by aiming our thoughts. It matters what we replace our negative thoughts with. Let me quote the apostle Paul again for an example of how we aim our thoughts. "Finally, brothers and sisters, whatever is true, whatever is noble, whatever is right, whatever is pure, whatever is lovely, whatever is admirable—if anything is excellent or praiseworthy—think about such things" (Philippians 4:8). Paul is aiming our thoughts, the way the Kieboom's staff aimed the men at the housefly.

Aim your thoughts higher. The simple act of looking up can change your mindset. In the book, *The Molecule of More: How a Single Chemical in Your Brain Drives Love, Sex, and Creativity—and Will Determine the Fate of the Human Race,* the authors begin the book by telling us to "look down." Then they ask, "What do you see? Your hands, your desk, your kitchen table, the floor, maybe a cup of coffee, or a laptop computer." They say these are the things you can touch, things you can control right now. Most of what you see when you look down is yours. Things in your possession. Then they tell us to "look up." Again, they ask, "What do you see? The ceiling, perhaps the sky, trees, clouds. Whatever is in the distance. To reach them you have to plan, think, calculate." It's unlike what we see when we look down. They go on to write:

> "Unlike what we see when we look down, the realm of *up* shows us things that we have to think about and work for in order to get.
>
> Sounds simple because it is. Yet to the brain this distinction is the gateway between two wildly different ways of thinking—two utterly different ways of dealing with the world. In your brain the *down* world is managed by a handful of chemicals—neurotransmitters, they're called— that let you experience satisfaction and enjoy whatever you have in the here and now. But when you turn your attention to the world of *up*, your brain relies on a different chemical—a single molecule—that not only allows you to move beyond the realm of what's at your fingertips, but also motivates you to pursue, to control, and to possess the world beyond your immediate grasp. It drives you to seek out these things far away, both physical things and things you cannot see, such as knowledge, love, and power.

Those down chemicals—call them the Here & Nows—
allow you to experience what is in front of you . . . The up
chemical is different. It makes you desire what you don't yet
have and drives you to seek new things . . . This chemical
in your brain is called dopamine. It is why we look in the
sky for redemption and God; it is why heaven is above and
earth is below . . . To your brain, this single molecule is the
ultimate multipurpose device, urging us, through thousands
of neurochemical processes, to move beyond the pleasure
of just being, into exploring the universe of possibilities
that come when we imagine."[126]

Looking up is how we will continue the change in our Automatic
System. We must get dopamine involved. Much of the time, we
never get out of the here and now thinking of the Automatic System.
It's concerned with the things we can control right now. But the
extrapersonal space of up deals with everything we can't touch unless
we move beyond our arm's length reach, whether it's three feet or three
million miles away. This is the realm of possibility.[127] Without it we will
not change the here and now, because the here and now is homeostasis.

The H&Ns deal with what we have. And, as we've seen, dopamine
deals with what we want and dopamine is not a bad thing when it hands
off the baton to the H&Ns. Matching our wants to our likes is critical.
But too many of us have stopped firing dopamine because we've given
up on a new life. We are stuck in the drudgery of the here and now.
This is the reason scripture tells us repeatedly to look up. We get our
eyes off of our possessions or lack thereof. We get our eyes up and it
fires dopamine—the chemical of possibility. And with this chemical,
we will change the Automatic System.

CHRIST OUTSIDE THE BOX

Christ performed miracles so He could show what was possible
when we move outside the box of a fixed mindset and into the realm of

possibility. One day He fed five thousand people with two fish and five loaves of bread. As evening approached that day, the disciples came to Him and said, "This is a remote place and it's already getting late. Send the crowds away, so they can go to the villages and buy themselves some food" (Matthew 14:15). Where they sensed trouble, Jesus saw possibility. But at eye level—using the H&N neurotransmitters—it didn't look like possibility. It looked like not enough. Christ had to show them how to participate with the Divine (theosis) using dopamine. "And he directed the people to sit down on the grass. Taking the five loaves and the two fish and looking up to heaven, he gave thanks and broke the loaves. Then he gave them to the disciples and the disciples gave them to the people" (Matthew 14:19). He leveled their eyesight first by making them sit down and then He put the need in front of them.

The disciples had boxed themselves into a world of measurement and could not see into the realm of possibility. We do the same thing. We look at the world at eye level and never look up into the world of possibility and only look at what our hands can grasp. This is why Jesus tells us not to worry about what we will wear and what we will eat. He directs our eyes up. He says, "Look at the birds of the air; they do not sow or reap or store away in barns and yet your heavenly Father feeds them" (Matthew 6:26). Jesus even said that He only does what He sees the Father doing (John 5:19). His eyes were ever looking up.

Where we look matters. Look too long at your possessions and they will possess you or make you feel hopeless, the way the disciples felt hopeless when offered five loaves and two fish. Because at eye level, we calculate our resources. The disciples looked outward and revealed need. Then Christ's upward look revealed strength and supply. It pushed their minds up and they participated in the Divine supply chain, which always comes from the realm of dopaminergic possibility. So, when you feel hopeless, the one simple act that you can do to change the chemistry in your brain is look up. "Set your minds on things above, not on earthly things" (Colossians 3:2). "So we fix our eyes not on what is seen, but on what is unseen, since what is seen is temporary, but what is unseen is eternal" (2 Corinthians 4:17-18). We move from a fixed mindset to a growth mindset when we set our minds on things above. Higher up, commonplace maxims are left behind. Possibility awaits at higher levels.

"(Dopamine) is the anticipation molecule . . . And if you want to feel it right now, if you want to put it in charge, you can do that. Look up."[128] Let's go higher with our thoughts and change the default settings of the Automatic System and think of what is possible.

REFLECTIONS

1. Spend the day with set times to look up and think about what is possible.

2. Next, spend the day with set times to look at life at eye level at the here and now.

3. How does looking up or looking eye level make you feel?

IDENTIFYING GOD IN THE BRAIN

The greater your knowledge of the goodness and grace of God in your life, the more likely you are to praise Him in the storm.

—MATT CHANDLER

Two men came to Miami from the Artic regions, where they had lived all their life. On the bus ride to the hotel, they passed one of the bays where some people were waterskiing. Having only seen kayaks and other hand-propelled boats throughout their lifetime, one man asked the other, "What makes the boat go so fast?" The other man watched for a few seconds, then replied, "Man on string push it."

When we enter a new mindset, we enter a new world—much like the men entering Miami from the Artic regions. It's hard to comprehend the new reality, so a mindset change requires a paradigm destruction, which is the shedding of the previous paradigm. Our fixed mindset rooted in religion must go.

The mindset of grace establishes a new system for the mind. "The ultimate object of the new mind is to enable us to understand and to appreciate the will of God in a way that wasn't possible before."[129] And to accomplish this, we must understand our present picture of God. Do you picture God as gracious and merciful or as punitive? Most of us see God both ways. When things are going great, we see a picture of God that is gracious and merciful. When we face adversity, our picture of God changes. Now we see a judgmental God. Maybe we even think He is mad at us and punishing us. But as long as we are switching back-and-forth between two pictures of God, then we never build a system that's rooted in the mindset of grace.

W. E. Hill,
"My Wife and My Mother-in-law."

Let me go further into this by showing you the old illusion "My Wife and My Mother-in-Law."[130]

What do you see? You may see a young woman with a bonnet looking away. Now try to find an old woman looking down and to the left. David Eagleman says that this is known as perceptual bi-stability. The lines on the page are consistent with two very different interpretations. When you stare at the figure, you'll see one version and then eventually the other.

"Here's the important part: nothing on the physical page changes . . . "[131]

When the image has flipped, it has to be because of something in the brain. Our brains have made a decision and, in this case, it doesn't have to be conscious. Our perceptual decision has been made in our visual system and the switchover is completely unconscious. This is how our brains crush ambiguity into choices.[132]

Why is this important? It proves our minds can unconsciously and seamlessly switch to a different perspective. It's a paradigm shift.

PARADIGM SHIFT
A fundamental change in approach or underlying assumptions; An important change that happens when the usual way of thinking about or doing something is replaced by a new and different way.

A NEW PICTURE

Being able to switch from a judgmental God to one that would desire His will for our life is a hard transformation for some of us. We always feel God is against us. We say, "Can His will really make us happy? It sounds like He will make me miserable. What's so good and pleasing about God's will?" We always want to be something other than what God wants us to be because we think God's will is either something out of reach or somewhat of a curse.

Most of the confusion in our lives comes from switching back-and-forth between a judgmental God to a merciful and gracious God. Either God is merciful and gracious, or He is punitive. Trying to hold both views in our belief system makes us unstable in all our ways. James 1:6–8 addresses this: "But when you ask, you must believe and not doubt, because the one who doubts is like a wave of the sea, blown and tossed by the wind. That person should not expect to receive anything from the Lord. Such a person is double-minded and unstable in all they do."

God is either for us or against us.

ONCE AND FOR ALL

By renewing our minds, we establish God's grace in our belief system. Think back to the prodigal son again. His paradigm choice was either being a hired servant or being a Jewish boy who tended pigs. One was based on an earlier version of himself, the other on a later version of himself—the one going home to the father. But he hadn't renewed himself. In his mind he had crushed ambiguity into a choice, but it wasn't a better choice. It was just the better of the two at the moment. It was reformation, not transformation. He had just chosen which bondage he was willing to live with. We do this when we confuse a God of condemnation with a God of mercy and grace. We will opt for reformation every time because the ego wants to remain in control. If we have a God of grace, then there's nothing for the ego to protect.

But we want to be our own god, which creates powerful resistance. We cling to the ego like a childhood security blanket, like birds to a tether. We just don't want to give up our securities, even when they are false and lead us to bondage. And the wrong picture of God ends up controlling our lives, because it's easier to think God is punitive. It's like a form of idolatry.

I think C.S. Lewis is right when he alludes to our transformation as being like the restoration of a house:

> "Imagine yourself as a living house. God comes in to rebuild that house. At first, perhaps, you can understand what He is doing. He is getting the drains right and stopping the leaks in the roof and so on: you knew that those jobs needed doing and so you are not surprised. But presently He starts knocking the house about in a way that hurts abominably and does not seem to make sense. What on earth is He up to? The explanation is that He is building quite a different house from the one you thought of—adding on a new wing here, putting on an extra floor there, running up towers, making courtyards. You thought you were going to be made into a decent little cottage: but He is building a palace. He intends to come and live in it Himself."[133]

This is the last thing the ego wants, so it resists by telling us that God is punishing us. It's like the man with one talent in Jesus's parable, who buried his talent because he felt his master was a harsh man. It's just another form of ego control. The ego ignores opportunity to learn and grow. Ego doesn't ask questions for fear of appearing weak. But Paul said, "I have been crucified with Christ and I no longer live, but Christ lives in me. The life I now live in the body, I live by faith in the Son of God, who loved me and gave himself for me" (Galatians 2:20).

Without an authentic picture of God settled in our minds, we won't participate with the Divine in our transformation. Do you think the prodigal son ever thought of his father as a punitive father after his father welcomed him home as a royal son? His picture of the father changed for good. The father's grace solidified it. Never again would he think his father would punish him and never again would the son want to leave home. This is what the death of Christ does for us. "But God demonstrates his own love for us in this: While we were still sinners, Christ died for us" (Romans 5:8).

So, to experience a paradigm shift, we first must experience a paradigm destruction. Discard the picture of God as a God of judgment and replace it with the picture of God as a God of mercy and love. Stopping switching between the two. For there is no condemnation for those who are in Christ Jesus" (Romans 8:1). Nothing new happens until we destroy the old paradigm.

This is mind renewal.

REFLECTIONS

1. Do you ever go back-and-forth in your mind between a picture of a judgmental God to a picture of a gracious and understanding God?

2. If you do switch back-and-forth, where did these pictures of God originate in your narrative?

THE SEEDS OF POSSIBILITY

Be what you are; realize what you are;
and proceed to show that you are what you are.
—D. MARTYN LLOYD-JONES

Seeing it for the first time, you'd think it was a joke. But it's an authentic monument to a real disaster that turned out to be a blessing, instead of a curse. The citizens of Enterprise, Alabama erected the monument in 1919 to honor the mighty boll weevil, an insect native to Mexico that first started destroying cotton crops in 1915 in the state. So why would they erect the statue as a tribute to a disaster? Well, there's a story behind the statue.

Boll Weevil Monument,
Enterprise, Alabama[281]

An enterprising citizen by the name of H. M. Sessions saw the boll weevil as an opportunity to convert the area to peanut farming and he convinced C. W. Baston, an indebted farmer, to back his venture. The first crop paid off their debts and soon other farmers followed. Even though cotton was grown again, the boll weevil taught farmers to diversify their crops. So, the monument was erected to the boll weevil as a tribute to how a group of farmers changed the narrative. A disaster became a blessing in disguise.

So, how did they get to the solution of peanut farming? They had to rethink their crops. **They looked inward and aligned themselves with their identity.** They were farmers, not just cotton farmers. They got outside the box of a fixed mindset that said it was cotton or nothing else. They had a paradigm shift and switched to a growth mindset that allowed them to learn and grow beyond cotton. The same must be true for us. We need to grow beyond our past failure and present crisis, beyond doom and gloom. So how did the farmers experience a paradigm shift?

Let's say you are one of those farmers in Alabama. How would you respond to the boll weevil? Would you be able to get cotton off your mind? Back then, it was deeply entrenched in not only their ways but in the fabric of their society. Cotton was the cash crop. And aren't cash crops hard to leave behind? Growing peanuts was untried and unknown. And when your hope is in the crop, then it doesn't much matter what you call yourselves. Cotton is king and the king rules. You just work for cotton. But when you are a farmer first and foremost, then you determine what goes in the ground. It's your choice. Again, it's what we do between stimulus and response that matters. We decide what to do next, but it takes identity awareness.

REIDENTIFY AND RESCRIPT

Think of the boll weevil as a script. What would its script be? Something like this: "I am destroying your crop and you can't stop me." Believing this message, the farmers would have collapsed into hopelessness. But give them credit. They said, "We are farmers and as farmers we can choose to grow a different crop." They never lost the vision of who they were. They were farmers with a choice. They refused to be the boll weevil's victim. James Clear writes, "Research has shown that once a person believes in a particular aspect of their identity, they are more likely to act in alignment with that belief."[134] There are reasons why this is true, because when we take action and make choices between stimulus and response that are based on identity, then it shapes the outcome.

Identity change was at the heart of the farmers' decision to grow peanuts. A peanut farmer is not a cotton farmer. But the one thing that remains the same is being a farmer. Most people can't transition into the person they want to become, because they believe identity is fixed. But identity is not only about what kind of farmer we want to become. It's about what kind of child of God we want to become. Then we plant the kinds of seeds that will define us. We reap what we sow (Galatians 6:8). So why are we still sowing cotton, so to speak, when it hasn't worked?

We never transform spiritually until we start sowing the right seeds for the kind of harvest we desire.

IN CHRIST

If you look at Paul's transition, Paul went from persecuting and hunting down Christians to becoming the greatest Christian the world has ever known. When Christ knocked him down and the scales fell off his eyes, Paul was a transformed man. He saw everything differently. He had a paradigm shift, or he had new eyes. This is why Paul used the phrase "in Christ" 164 times. He understood Christ as being within the believer. He knew change started with identity with Christ and this changed the outcome of his life.

When we participate in the identity of Christ, then we step outside the box of doom and gloom and into the space of possibility. Just as the farmers stepped outside the box of planting only cotton. Their identity as farmers shaped the outcome. They chose what crop to plant that would steer them away from destruction. Identity shapes our choices. Identity doesn't take our choice away. It strengthens and focuses it on possibility. What is possible for you? What do you want to become?

Identifying ourselves as being in Christ is a key concept. Why does this matter? It matters because when we see with the eyes of Christ, then we see what He is doing, then we do it. Jesus told His followers: "Very truly I tell you, the Son can do nothing by himself; he can do only what he sees his Father doing, because whatever the Father does the Son also does" (John 5:19). Paul put it like this: "Set your minds on things above, not on earthly things. For you died and your life is now hidden with Christ in God" (Colossians 3:2–3). Paul says elsewhere, "For me to live is Christ" (Philippians 1:2). He wrote this to the Galatians: ". . . It is no longer I who live, but Christ who lives in me . . ." (Galations 2:20 NKJV).

Let's call this the mindset of Christ. When we enter the mindset of Christ, the rules change in the world. We judge everything in the light of grace. We make choices about our identity based upon grace. We leave the world of measurements where we measure ourselves against the world. How much beauty do I possess? How much money? How much fame? How much success? This is how the fixed mindset measures our worth.

The mindset of Christ sets our minds on things above. Then we act in alignment with Christ. The way to know when we've entered the mindset of Christ is when we set our minds on things above, the way Jesus only did what He saw His Father doing. We get out of the world of guilt and condemnation. Becoming whole is better than being broken. We see things differently. Wouldn't it be nice just to have confidence that all things will turn out the way God intends? We can trust in His help, not His judgment. This reinterprets everything. It changes the rules of engagement. Entering the mindset of Christ unleashes grace. It's being able to see ourselves through the lens of Christ's love and not through the lens of guilt and condemnation.

We like the sound of grace, but most of us have a hard time letting go and really believing in grace. We feel so helpless at the throne of grace because nothing is required of us. Nothing in our hands or in our bank accounts can purchase grace. Grace is outside the realm of measurements—where we are no longer measured by a failure. In the mindset of Christ, we are not defined by where we have been, mistakes we've made, the setbacks we've had, the inadequacies that we've struggled with, the old paradigms of who we think we are. Rather, we are defined by where we are going and who we are becoming.

We understand that Christ is our paradigm. We believe Christ is dwelling within us, that we are together, that we are one. Now you talk about a different mindset!

I realized when I met Christ some years after my car wreck that I could see life differently, that I must see life differently. Because I couldn't see it before because fear had blinded me. But I had to observe the ego to defeat it, then I became new in the attitude of my mind (Ephesians 4:23). And Paul says that the old self never sees the world as being a place of learning and growing. The old self maintains the deceit that judgment is just around the corner, not life abundant.

We must see Christ in everyone and everything—and I will take it a step further—we must participate with the Divine at the center of our identity (theosis). This is the paradigm of Christ. His vision gives us hope for the future. Mindfulness of Christ's identity creates the ability to see new things in significant ways. This gets at the heart of a paradigm shift. This is the lens. When I am transformed, I can now see with the eyes of Christ and feel with the heart of Christ. This is ultimate meaning—in Christ. Then our paradigm shifts. Christ creates a sense of dignity, integrity, and character. Not because we are worthy of it, but because our worth is based on grace. And self-acceptance is grace turned inward. Nothing will change if our fixed mindset remains in the accusatory mode and tells us the future is hopeless.

When we make choices between stimulus and response that are based on our identity in Christ then it takes us out of the world of judgment. Then we can choose the life we've always wanted without feeling guilt and condemnation.

CHANGE IS NOT A FEELING

Change is acting in alignment with our belief, which shapes the final outcome. The farmers believed in their ability to farm a new crop. One bad crop would not be able to define them. They reached for a new seed. They made a choice in the land of possibility. They took a risk and succeeded.

What new seed do you want to plant? In Christ all things are possible. Paul said, "I can do all things through Christ who strengthens me" (Philippians 4:13). So, choose your seed of possibility. To further this, I'd like to leave you with something written by Thomas Merton that I believe sums up what I've attempted to say in this chapter:

> "The mind that is the prisoner of conventional ideas and the will that is captive of its own desire cannot accept the seeds of an unfamiliar truth and a supernatural desire. For how can I receive the seeds of freedom if I am in love with slavery and how can I cherish the desire of God if I am filled with another and an opposite desire? God cannot plant His liberty in me because I am a prisoner and I do not even desire to be free. I love my captivity and I imprison myself in the desire for the things that I hate and I have hardened my heart against true love. I must learn therefore to let go of the familiar and the usual and consent to what is new and unknown to me. I must learn to "leave myself" in order to find myself by yielding to the love of God. If I were looking for God, every event and every moment would sow, in my will, grains of His life that would spring up one day in a tremendous harvest.

> If these seeds would take root in my liberty and if His will would grow from my freedom, I would become the love that He is and my harvest would be His glory and my own joy . . . We do not detach ourselves from things in order to attach ourselves to God, but rather we become detached from ourselves in order to see and use all things in and for God."[135]

REFLECTION

1. Do you react to your mistakes by wanting to protect your self-image?

2. When you make a mistake, do you identify more with the voice of accusation or the voice of possibility?

3. Do you believe Christ is living at the center of your being?

STRIKING AT THE ROOT OF OUR LIES

Yes, the mind seeks truth, but it can also create lies.

—RICHARD ROHR

After only a few years of marriage, a young man and his wife were at each other's throat. The wife was distraught and had decided the only way to save their struggling marriage was to try counseling. She felt it was their last straw. When they arrived at the counselor's office, the counselor jumped right in and opened the floor for discussion.

"What seems to be the problem?" Immediately, the husband hung his head without anything to say. On the other hand, the wife began talking incessantly for twenty minutes, describing all the wrongs within their marriage. Just non-stop complaints about their marriage. When the wife finally paused, the counselor went over, picked her up by her shoulders and kissed her passionately for several minutes. Then sat her back down.

The wife and husband sat there stunned and speechless.

After a long pause, the counselor looked over at the husband and said, "Your wife NEEDS that at least twice a week!"

The husband blinked hard, scratched his head, and replied, "I can have her here every Tuesday and Thursday."

He wasn't taking responsibility for the part he played in his marriage. For this man, change was outside him and not within. He had very little self-awareness. He wasn't willing to strike at the root of the problem in his marriage.

To change any situation, we must first change ourselves. Remember what Stephen Covey wrote, "We can only achieve quantum improvements in our lives as we quit hacking at the leaves of attitude and behavior and get to work on the root, the paradigms from which our attitudes and behaviors flow."[136] In other words, we must stop being controlled by outer forces and look within to where real change is possible—by taking responsibility for our actions and striking at the root. Most of us never pay attention to what we need to be paying attention to, because like the husband, we are controlled by our own biases. We aren't seeing the root clearly.

Let's see how this works. First, take a look at the two tables below that I've adapted from Roger N. Shepard:[137]

Thaler and Sunstein write about this table illusion in their book, *Nudge*, "Suppose that you are thinking about which one would work better as a coffee table in your living room. What would you say are the dimensions of the two tables? Take a

Roger N. Shepard. *"Turning the Tables,"* Mind Sights, 1990.

guess at the ratio of the length to the width of each. Just eyeball it."[138]

If you see these two tables as different, you are human. But the fact is: they are both the same. Measure them if you'd like. The two tabletops are identical.

There are systematic biases in the way we think. Thaler and Sunstein believe: "More recently, psychologists have come to understand that these heuristics and biases emerge from the interplay between the Automatic System and the Reflective System."[139] Let's take a look at how these biases form faulty beliefs and behavior.

OUR DEFAULT SETTINGS

Think of our mindsets as the Automatic System's default setting. Our default setting goes in one of two directions: toward overconfidence or toward insecurity. We always think we are more capable than we are or less capable than we are. We see ourselves as more superior than others or as more inferior to others. Both overconfidence and inferiority stem from the Automatic System's default settings, which are attached to the patterns of this world (Romans 12:2).

On one end of the spectrum is insecurity, on the other end is overconfidence (pride). Of course, there are all points in-between. And I think we can waffle back-and-forth between overconfidence and insecurity, depending on the adversity we face. But mostly, we view life through one of these two biases that are attached to the patterns of the world. Also, these two extremes are prominent in a fixed mindset. Eventually we get trapped by our biases.

So, I need new eyes and even new ears to see past the biases of the world. Jesus said, "Do you have eyes but fail to see and ears but fail to hear?"[140] Jesus understood mindsets hinder our vision and hearing. We get pigeonholed. But new eyes and ears give us a different way to think, feel, and act.

First, **we are prone to insecurity because of an overactive inner critic that keeps reminding us of our failures and weaknesses**. Let me take you back to my car wreck. After my car wreck, my default setting was insecurity. Every car ride felt like the car wreck would happen again. I interpreted every event as if it might be my last. I made every decision about the future through the lens of insecurity. My fear kept me bound for years. Insecurity became my paradigm—my lens upon which I viewed the world. I kept committing *confirmation bias*— seeing what I expected to see.[141] We perpetuate a confirmation bias of seeing what we expect to see when we're not open to growth and transformation. We are in fight-or-flight mode. We are not implementing the observer effect.

FIGHT-OR-FLIGHT MODE
Acute stress reaction that occurs when in the presence of something mentally or physically terrifying.

PRIDE COMES BEFORE THE FALL

The second default setting is overconfidence (pride). Adam Grant writes, "Yes, some of this comes down to our fragile egos. We're driven to deny our weaknesses when we want to see ourselves in a positive light or paint a glowing picture of ourselves to others. The less intelligent we are in a particular domain, the more we seem to overestimate our actual intelligence in that domain."[142] We always exaggerate our virtues, which leads to self-delusion. When prisoners serving time for assault, robbery, fraud, and other crimes were asked to compare themselves with the general population, they rated themselves as being moral and honest and also more compassionate and self-controlled. There was just one quality they rated below the general population. When it came to being law-abiding, they rated themselves as only average.[143]

When we are overconfident, the orbitofrontal cortex—which is the region of the brain that pieces together all the information that we need to make decisions and in regulating our emotions—becomes less active.[144] Being overconfident means we aren't having deep thoughts or emotion regulation. When we don't put in the effort to change our perspective, we tend to be overconfident,[145] because we think we already know what we need to know. The *desirability bias* comes into play—we see what we want to see. It's akin to confirmation bias. Think of gambler's tendency to explain away their losses, which permits them to believe their chances of winning are higher than they really are. They miss the pattern that their losses are adding up and they go blindly into failure and loss. They keep going because they see what they want to see.

DESIRABILITY BIAS

Exaggerating one's positive traits; Overestimating one's degree
of control in life; Overly optimistic beliefs about future events

CONFIRMATION BIAS

The tendency of people to favor information that confirms or
strengthens their beliefs or values.

OPTIMISM BIAS

The inclination to overestimate the likelihood of encountering
positive events in the future and to underestimate the likelihood
of experiencing negative events.

In fact, we're all prone to overestimate our abilities. We all know
we are dying but still believe it will happen to someone else. We
have a false sense of security on the highway because we consider
ourselves above-average drivers and expect our skill to protect us, even
though many accidents are caused by factors beyond our control. This
"optimism bias" causes us to underestimate the risk of some types of
negative events occurring in our lives. The toxic combination of fear
and overconfidence leads to bad choices.[146]

Psychologists call an overriding confidence in our own thoughts,
feelings, and intentions the *introspection illusion*.[147] We overestimate
the extent to which our actions depend on our own will. It's flattering
and empowering to believe we are in control, that we can will the
outcome to happen, but that is false. One of the most hilarious and
pitiful scenes from the Exodus is when the children of Israel were
readying to leave Egypt. They had assembled themselves into an army
with makeshift weaponry. They were ready to be a warring nation. But
the account in Exodus 13:17–18 reads: "When Pharaoh let the people
go, God did not lead them on the road through the Philistine country,

though that was shorter. For God said, 'If they face war, they might change their minds and return to Egypt.' So God led the people around by the desert road toward the Red Sea. The Israelites went up out of Egypt ready for battle." They couldn't perceive their own weakness, so God said, "Fine, I'm not going to argue with you. If you're ready for battle, let's go. But I don't think so." Then He led them around any possibility of war early on. He took them on the roundabout way. And the roundabout way is always better than our own way.

INTROSPECTION ILLUSION
A cognitive bias in which one wrongly thinks they have direct insight into the origins of their mental states, while treating others' introspections as unreliable.

SELECTIVE EDITING

When we decide that the result will be overly positive or overly negative, then we accept as valid only data that brings about this conclusion. Dr. Arthur Freeman and Rose DeWolf, in their book, *Woulda, Coulda, Shoulda,* tell us to imagine a scientist who analyzes water and notices only the hydrogen atoms but not the oxygen, or finds the oxygen and overlooks the hydrogen. This *selective editing* is analysis created from our biases. We see only the pieces of information that lead us to a preconceived conclusion.[148] We see only what we expect to see, want to see, and are ready to see.

SELECTIVE EDITING
Ignoring evidence that conflicts with a preconceived view.

It happened to Jesus's disciples. They kept *seeing* what they expected to see and wanted to see, which was a political Messiah that would overthrow the Roman government and usher in a new earthly kingdom to replace it. When Jesus told Peter He must go to Jerusalem and die, Peter had an interesting response. "Peter took him aside and began to rebuke him. 'Never, Lord!' he said. 'This shall never happen to you'" (Matthew 16:22). Peter suffered from confirmation bias. He could only see what he expected to see—a political Messiah. He misunderstood the Messiah's kingdom was a heavenly kingdom, as most did in those days before the Resurrection. For Peter to understand, he would need a paradigm shift. It took the Resurrection to nudge him out of his biases.

It is true in science as it is in spirituality that what one sees— actually or metaphorically—depends on what one looks for and what one expects. Think again of the maids who interpreted their work as exercise. When they were nudged by the experimenters to believe their work was improving their health, the results were amazing. Just thought alone.

Thoughts based on flawed beliefs can create problems for us. When we only see our world through biases, then we never become self-aware. Why is self-awareness so important? It leads us to truth that will set us free. We let go of our illusions.

In our next session, we will discuss how to reset the default settings. For now, let's reflect on and discuss our biases.

REFLECTIONS

1. Have you ever edited out the negative and expected to see
   something—just because you wanted to see it so bad you were not
   looking at all of the evidence? For example ignoring a health issue
   or ignoring the negative in a relationship.

2. What perceptions about yourself and your current situation are you
   agreeing to that keep you from experiencing a paradigm shift?

3. Are you seeing what you expect to see or what you want to see and
   avoiding the truth of your situation?

CHANGING OUR FACTORY SETTINGS

If you want small changes in your life, work on your attitude.
But if you want big and primary changes, work on your paradigm.

—STEPHEN COVEY

There was once a dirt road in Canada back in Model T days that was muddy in the summer and frozen into crusty grooves or tracks in the winter. Beside the road was a road sign that warned drivers: "Choose carefully which rut you drive in, you'll be in it for the next 20 miles."

The same is true about our brains. There are ruts or grooves in the brain that our memories have traveled for years. In fact, brain "activity flows through the system based on what happened before."[149] Think of it as a rut in your mind. So, we tend to think the same thing repeatedly because it has become an unavoidable rut. We are really responding to what has happened in the past. This is the deception of an unconscious habit.

Our "brains begin with many possible routes through the neural networks; with time, the practiced pathways become difficult to exit. Unused pathways become thinned away. Neurons that can't find success with the world eventually fold up shop and (die)."[150] This creates our fixed mindset and we become unwilling to change our perspectives because we've chosen to travel the path of least resistance for years and this path created the same thoughts, the same feelings, and the same behavior. In short, we get stuck in the rut of a fixed mindset and in this mindset, we have the tendency to think negative thoughts of insecurity, or we self-inflate and think thoughts of overconfidence. Because when stress increases, we are more likely to search for confirming information and to ignore information that is inconsistent with our expectations.[151]

WHAT STRESS DOES TO THE MIND

Our Automatic Systems double down on the path of least resistance under stress. We stop deep thinking and overlook difficult decision making. It works like this: "When the fear center of the brain (amygdala) is activated and is not calmed, it triggers a cascade of caustic events, which ravages our bodies and brains. The sympathetic nervous system activates the release of stress hormones . . . "[152] This in turn stops a protein that's a brain-derived neurotrophic factor, which makes neurons grow strong. "Think of it as fertilizer for your neurons."[153] Our brains can even make new neurons under the influence of such proteins, which causes us to learn faster and easier. "When this protein and other proteins like it are unavailable, the brain stops making new neurons and the neurons we have begin to wither and die."[154] The fight-or-flight response shuts down growth. It actually creates the fixed mindset. We can't grow and transform while we are in a state of fear and insecurity. Growth is arrested and neurons die. It's the Popeye syndrome, "I am what I am."

POPEYE SYNDROME
"I am what I am." A belief that we cannot change. An excuse that keeps us trapped in bad habits that we have created.

As we've learned in the last chapter, insecurity and overconfidence are our factory settings of a fixed mindset. Factory settings are what happen when we choose to do nothing. Think of the screen lock on your phone. The factory established a default setting. Say you decide to change the screen lock factory setting from three minutes of inactivity before it locks to five minutes of inactivity before the it locks. You access the factory settings options and choose a new default. If you're happy with the factory setting, then you do nothing else. A factory setting in the brain can be changed—that's the good news. But the Reflective System gets lazy and runs the Automatic System's factory setting without questioning the results. Or the Reflective System can be overwhelmed by stress and just shut down.

Resetting our factory setting is how we create a new starting point for new thought processes. The Reflective System can interrupt and make changes in the unconscious network. Remember how Kutol changed the script of Play-Doh and created a fresh start? Making a fresh start begins with a decision to change our script from this point forward.

This is where our study will move into how our narratives impact our potential for lasting change.

OUR NARRATIVE IMPACTS LASTING CHANGE

I'll take you back to the life of Moses to point out how hard a fresh start was for him. Forty years before the burning bush, Moses had killed a man in Egypt that was abusing an Israelite slave. "Looking this way and that and seeing no one, he killed the Egyptian and hid him in the sand" (Exodus 2:12). Now fast-forward forty years and God gives him a new mission. He didn't act on God's will, instead, it appears he chose to do nothing.[155] He traveled the path of least resistance, which led to insecurity and doubt. He doubted God's will because he couldn't resolve the past in his mind.

After the burning bush encounter, he returned home and spoke with his father-in-law about leaving and returning to Egypt. His father-in-law gave him his blessings. But Moses didn't leave for Egypt—it would seem that Moses was still reluctant.[156] He drifted around thinking about his old narrative. How do we know? Because God came to him again and said, "Go back to Egypt, for all those who wanted to kill you are dead" (Exodus 4:19). God knew what Moses was thinking. Moses still feared the consequences of his earlier life. He was seeing what he expected to see—someone back in Egypt who was ready to settle an old score. He interpreted the future in reference to his past. But God assured him that all was well. His old narrative would not come back to haunt him. He had to let the past be the past, which is fundamental to experiencing a paradigm shift. Moses had to choose a new beginning, but he was stuck because he couldn't see the big picture. He was focused on the past and it had him moping around in the desert with no goal motivation. How could he be a deliverer if he was once a murderer? He kept ruminating on the past failure of killing an Egyptian and it held him in a fixed mindset. He had to separate his failed past from his present self. **He had to choose a big picture view of life.** And the same goes for us.

We learn what to do or we learn what not to do in the future based on what we were rewarded for doing in the past or—in the case of Moses—punished for doing in the past. Going back to the scene of the crime seemed like punishment to Moses, not a recommission and reward. His brain didn't detect any relevance to reward. No acetylcholine was being produced and remember that acetylcholine tells the brain what's important to pay attention to and pursue. He wasn't motivated to return due to a sense of punishment. "Feelings of pleasure and disappointment are part of the feedback mechanism that helps your brain distinguish useful actions from useless ones."[157]

Moses's larger goal at that moment was to avoid punishment. And his not moving forward led to regret. We avoid facing the future and moving on, avoiding repairing the past, which is futile. This is reformation, not transformation. In reformation, we try to predict the future using an old reward or an old punishment. Punishment causes us to avoid or suppress certain situations. Then we commit selective-editing.

What is the path into believing and then seeing the big picture? The path has everything to do with our goals. And what changes our goals is value.

How do we find the path towards understanding the broader perspective? This path is intricately linked to our goals and what defines our goals is value.

THE PATH TO A NEW FUTURE

To change a goal, we must first remove our sense of punishment. When our focus remains solely on our problems, our motivation isn't driven by value. Moses lacked a big picture view because he limited his future by a sense of past punishment. Richard Rohr writes, "You cannot really love reality with the judgmental mind, because you'll always try to control it, fix it, or understand it before you give yourself to it."[158] Moses felt his return to Egypt would include punishment for what he'd done. He wasn't ready to make a fresh start because he remained fixated on the past. Studies have proven that when reward is withheld, our brains disengage. The brain basically says, "Why should I give energy to something that doesn't reward my effort?"

A fixed mindset of guilt and condemnation leaves us no choice between stimulus and response. Everything is set in stone, so we don't even attempt change. Redemption isn't possible because what has happened to us has determined who we are. We lose our ability to choose a response.[159] Then everything becomes unconscious and automatic and the pain of our hopelessness leads to our unhealthy attachments. "I am what I am. So, I might as well give up and give in to hopelessness."

Moses had thought these thoughts for so long they were automatic. It took his Reflective System's involvement to change his Automatic System. How did this happen? He realized his past wasn't going to come back and haunt him. This is so fundamental to changing our habits. We must stop thinking old thoughts that lead to painful memories.

Research has proven that when people are prompted with positive stimuli, they do better at creative tasks. They literally see the bigger picture. Their eyes sweep a wider field of vision instead of just focusing on what's straight ahead, as they do when prompted with negative stimuli. One of the most influential ideas in positive psychology is what has become known as the "broaden and build" theory: Positive emotions broaden your perspective and enable you to build skills that help you flourish both personally and professionally.[160] Being positive offers us the bigger picture. Being negative narrows our vision, the way it did with Moses. He got tripped up by the past.

BROADEN AND BUILD THEORY

Positive emotions (such as happiness, interest and anticipation) broaden one's awareness and encourage novel, exploratory thoughts and actions.

Thinking back on painful memories, brings up the painful emotions making them the dominant emotions we carry into the future. Think of the man with one talent in Jesus's parable. He buried his talent because he had a big picture of his master's punishment, which turned out to be false (Matthew 25:14-30). How long will we keep punishing ourselves? How long will we let shame rule and reign?

A growth mindset is this: If we've failed in business, we try again. If we've failed in marriage, we try again. If we've failed our children, we try again. If we've failed in our pursuit of success, we try again. But know this: attempting transformation may feel like punishment before it feels like reward. This is why people aren't motivated to achieve their aspirations. We are more apt to want to repair what we did in the past, rather than accepting a fresh start.

Moses had to decide to grow beyond his failure and he did so by adopting a big picture view of things. He stopped comparing his old self to his future self. Thinking about past memories, brings up past emotions that are tied to the past memory. In this way, we are bringing these old emotions into our present situation.

ENVISIONING YOUR FUTURE

The big picture of who you are based on God's unconditional love is fundamental to hope and change. Without a vision, you will perish (Proverbs 29:18). I believe this means a vision of your authentic self in Christ. You must have a vision, a big picture—I'll even describe it as a lens to look through—of what the authentic, free you will look like. You will need to think "big picture." Who could you be, if you were totally free from the past?

In that famous pre-battle speech in the movie *Braveheart*, William Wallace says, "Run and you'll live—at least a while. And dying in your beds many years from now, would you be willing to trade all the days from this day to that for one chance, just one chance to come back here and tell our enemies that they may take our lives, but they'll never take our freedom!"[161]

The question we must ask ourselves is: Who do we long to be? Then craft a vision based on unconditional love. Think of it as aiming your life. It takes courage to cocreate with God a vision of authenticity that will lead to transformation. Abandon your sense of guilt and condemnation and become vulnerable to God. You will not find rebuke. You will be recommissioned as Moses was. Why settle for anything less than an authentic vision of the big picture of your life?

Have courage to step into your story and set big picture goals, even if failure has been a major part of your past. Changing the factory settings of overconfidence and insecurity is a critical step in making a fresh start. We take off the false self we've fashioned for the world's eyes and put on the new transformed self that has an authentic vision of our inner life. Who do you want to become?

REFLECTIONS

1. What is your most prominent memory in the story of your life?

2. Do you keep returning to a moment of trauma anytime stressful events occur?

3. Do you have a tendency to want to repair the past or are you able to make a fresh start when you fail?

NOTHING IS EVER WRITTEN THAT CAN'T BE REWRITTEN

WHO'S TELLING THE STORY?

Never be in a hurry; do everything quietly and in a calm spirit.
Do not lose your inner peace for anything whatsoever,
even if your whole world seems upset.

—SAINT FRANCIS DE SALES

Children have their security blankets and stuffed animals to help with sleep at night. And Chris Hurn's son was no different. This is why the alarm was sounded when his beloved stuffed giraffe, named Joshie, had gone missing after they returned home from spending a few days at the Ritz-Carlton on Amelia Island in Florida. Chris's son was distraught and it was determined that Joshie must have been left behind at the Ritz-Carlton. First Chris told his son, "Joshie is fine. He's just taking an extra long vacation at the resort." His son seemed to buy it and was finally able to fall asleep, albeit Joshie-less for the first time in a long while.

That very night, the Ritz-Carlton called to tell Chris that they had Joshie. Thankfully, he had been found in the laundry and was handed over to the hotel's Loss Prevention Team. Chris came clean to the staff about the story he had told his son and asked if they would mind taking a picture of Joshie on a lounge chair by the pool to substantiate his fabricated story. The Loss Prevention Team said they'd do it and he hung up the phone very relieved.

A couple days went by and they received a package from the hotel. It was his son's giraffe, Joshie, along with some Ritz-Carlton-branded "goodies" (a frisbee, football, etc.). Also included in the package was a binder full of pictures that meticulously documented Joshie's extended stay at the Ritz. The first picture was Joshie wearing shades by the pool (Chris's original request/suggestion), another showed Joshie driving a golf cart. Others captured him hanging with the hotel parrot, getting a massage in the spa (with cucumber slices covering his eyes) and one of him monitoring the security cameras in the control room. They even made a security badge for Joshie. Hurn wrote a blog post about the incident that went viral. Everyone loved the story about a hotel going above and beyond to help a little boy overcome misplacing his beloved Joshie.[162] So, here's my question: In the future, when having to decide where to go on another vacation, will the Hurns consider returning to the Ritz-Carlton? You bet they will! Why? The answer may surprise you. Let's dive deeper into what Daniel Kahneman calls the *experiencing self* and the *remembering self* to discover why the Hurns would choose the Ritz-Carlton again.

EXPERIENCING SELF

The *you* in the moment that experiences life.

REMEMBERING SELF

The *you* that writes the story. The story it tells us is not always true as it has a tendency to disqualify the positive.

When we remember the experiences of our lives, we remember our experience in story form. Daniel Kahneman writes, "Memories are all we get to keep from our experiences of living and the only perspective that we can adopt as we think about our lives is therefore that of the remembering self."[163] The experiencing self is the "you" in the moment that experiences life. The remembering self is the "you" that writes the history. It is also the remembering self that is consulted when planning the future. "The experiencing self is the one that answers the question: 'Does it hurt now?' The remembering self is the one that answers the question: 'How was it, on the whole?'"[164] And it's the remembering self that needs our attention, because the story it tells us is not always true. It has biases. It doesn't always tell the story truthfully and this is where shame-based, fear-based paradigms originate, because the remembering self and the experiencing self don't always agree on what happened.

Our remembering self has the tendency to disqualify the positive and chooses to tell a different story, so the remembering self is where the emptying out will occur and then we replace the old, false narrative with the narrative that more represents the truth. Let's see why the two selves don't always agree on what happened.

REFRAMING THE PAST

Let's go back to the Joshie story at the beginning. Remember, I asked if the Hurns would choose to return to the Ritz-Carlton? Would they return because the hotel took such great care of returning Joshie with a binder of pictures? Or would they return because rules of memory would determine their choice, just as it had in the above experiment? A bad experience—losing Joshie—was capped off with a great experience of returning Joshie with a story of an extended vacation. Now which part of their experience will they remember? Losing Joshie or getting Joshie home?

For the sake of argument, let's say the Ritz-Carlton's Loss Prevention Team couldn't locate Joshie. Joshie was lost. Joshie wasn't coming home. How would this predict their likelihood of returning to the Ritz-Carlton on Amelia Island? Wouldn't it be like returning to the scene of a crime? Old memories of devastation and loss would rule. So, we can safely say the Hurns would choose a new destination based on how this vacation ended—no matter how much fun in the sun they experienced.

Remember, memories are all we get to keep from our experience of living and the remembering self is the one telling the story. To change your old narrative, we need to ask why the remembering self wants to tell this story, whether it be a story of shame and loss or one of triumph and return.

Our old narratives may be telling us a bad story or a good story because the episode of our life ended horribly or ended in triumph like Joshie's story. For our study we will focus on the old narratives that didn't end so well, because this is what keeps us from letting ourselves be loved by God and by others. It's all a matter of what part of the story the remembering self is telling us and if it's choosing to remind us of the ending that may disqualify the positive within the event it has recorded.

When we go through a divorce, the remembering self records the horrible breakup, therefore, when we remember our marriage, we remember the shame and disappointment of it, even though there may have been ten wonderful years, because the very critical part of a story is how it ends. This is called the peak-end rule. It's described like this: "Our memory has evolved to represent the most intense moment of an episode of pain or pleasure (the peak) and the feelings when the episode was at its end."[165] The peak-end is where the remembering self chooses to add more weight. Think of any good movie you've enjoyed and it's probably a favorite because of the way it ended. And we can apply this to any event in our lives. If we succeed in business, only to have it erased by an economic downturn, then we will feel like a failure, even though we built an incredible company.

PEAK-END RULE
Judging an experience largely based on how you feel at its peak and at its end, rather than based on the total sum or average of every moment of the experience..

The remembering self tells the story of heartbreak and shame if this is the way the story ended. So, we must tell the story more faithfully, which means we have to go back inside the narrative and remember it again and rewrite the ending, because until we do, then we will accept the lie the remembering self is telling us about that part of our lives.

Research professor and author, Brené Brown, says, "When we have the courage to walk into our story and own it, we get to write the ending. And when we don't own our stories of failure, setbacks, and hurt—they own us."[166] This is why going back through our old narratives is so important. We must tell the story more faithfully. This means we must ask ourselves, "What emotion is telling the story?"

RECOGNIZE WHAT EMOTION IS TELLING THE STORY

We must first identify what emotion is telling our story. Odds are we've been listening to the remembering self's story for so long that we don't even realize there's an emotion attached to it. We have so internalized the message that it has become our identity. Remember the quote from James Clear writes, "Over time, the cues that spark our habits become so common that they are essentially invisible. For this reason, we must begin the process of behavior change with awareness."[167] If we aren't aware of the unconscious cues, then we run on autopilot. Running on autopilot means we are living in the past. So, my question to you is: What part of the story is the remembering self telling—the good part or the bad ending?

Miriam Greenspan writes, "When you are in pain, you tend to resort to your core defect story as an explanation for (the pain)." The old narrative explains why we should feel shame or guilt. It reminds us of why we are weak and sad.

We need small victories to change the old narrative. If what we remember about our lives is dictated by the peak-end rule, as Kahneman believes, then new peaks must be established to replace the old. This is what Romans 12:2 means when it says we should no longer conform to the old patterns of the world. We renew our minds with better patterns and create higher peaks by cocreating with God a new ending. We achieve this new ending by paying attention to our thoughts and narratives and immediately reframing with a positive outcome with God. We are recreating our reality every day by changing what we believe and see, ultimately choosing what we believe and do. Christ changed the ending. Life doesn't end with death, but with resurrection power. ". . . then the saying that is written will come true" (1 Corinthians 15:54). Isn't this the power of the gospel? Isn't this the good news? "Death has been swallowed up in victory" (1 Corinthians 15:54 NIV).

To change our narrative, we must change the direction of our lives. We must reframe a negative ending into something positive.

Let's go back to the story of Chris Hurn's son and Joshie. Their vacation ended with losing Joshie, but the staff at the Ritz-Carlton had a new ending in mind. Joshie wasn't lost. Joshie was on an extended vacation and sent pictures to prove it. To change our narrative, we must change what we think about what we feel. Miriam Greenspan writes, "Psychologists call changing what you think about what you feel—'cognitive restructuring' or 'reframing.' For instance, thinking 'I'm weak' when you feel sad or scared can be reframed as 'I'm strong and courageous enough to let myself feel sad or scared.'"[168] This may sound like a mental trick, but it's actually a form of power. It's the power of vulnerability. Instead of being defeated by the pain, we tell ourselves how we will overcome, in spite of the pain.

To find the positive in your future, read the Bible. It is full of prophecies or predictions about your future. The prophetic words tell us how things will end. A prophecy is like a North Star—it gives you direction, guidance, stability and purpose. It reveals what God will do in the future. It takes you back to God's promises.

WHO IS TELLING OUR STORY?

In a recent essay Paul Ricoeur claimed that we learn to become the narrator and the hero of our own story, without actually becoming the author of our own life. We can live in the false self and thereby only remember the bad stuff in our past. All because we spend too much time trying to make sense of failure. Regret is an odd energy. The reason we are studying the false self and the true self is because one or the other tells our story. If the false self tells our story, then it has biases. It wants control and the ego tells lies to maintain it. Some have called it the *personal historian*,[169] which serves the functions of observing (perceiving) and recording (remembering) personal experience. And as the personal historian, it fabricates and revises history. It either takes credit for success while denying responsibility for failure, or it sinks us in total despair. It goes back to our factory settings of overconfidence or insecurity.

PERSONAL HISTORIAN
Observing and recording personal experience with one of three cognitive biases: "egocentricity (self perceived as more central to events than it is), beneffectance (self perceived as selectively responsible for desired but not undesired outcomes), and conservatism (resistance to cognitive change)."[170]

One study shows that people can adopt two different visual perspectives when remembering an event: Field memories (i.e., first-person memories) are visualized as if one is looking through one's own eyes; observer memories (i.e., third-person memories) are visualized as if one is looking at oneself through the eyes of a bystander.[171]

FIELD MEMORIES
The memory point of view that we occupied when we first experienced something.

OBSERVER MEMORIES

The memory point of view that we did not occupy when we first experienced it, but rather see ourselves in the remembered scene.

Observer memories disconnect the past self and the future self. Studies have shown that blaming past behavior on situational forces creates the potential to behave in the same way again, given the same circumstances. On the other hand, attributing past behavior to an old self (feeling responsible) suggests that if the same circumstances arise again, the new self will act differently because the new self is not choosing a response based on the past.[172] That old self is not me. Isn't this Paul's point when he writes, "You were taught, with regard to your former way of life, to put off your old self, which is being corrupted by its deceitful desires; to be made new in the attitude of your mind; and to put on the new self, created to be like God in true righteousness and holiness" (Ephesians 4:22-24). We must—once and for all—put off the old self. We must build a connection with the new self and act on its behalf. Now we are ready to lay down some richer memories. But first let's review the influence of the peak-end rule.

REFLECTIONS

1. Describe an event in your past where you felt you experienced a failure and the peak-end rule.

2. Now rethink this event and look at it as if you are a bystander (third-person memory) and not a personal historian with a first-person memory. Do you discover new realities? Do you discover that you may have disqualified the positive?

HOW BAD IS BAD?

When an inner situation is not made conscious,
it appears outside as fate.

—CARL JUNG

W e all agree that life is difficult. Bad can be very bad. Thinking of how bad things can go in life, I remembered this newspaper ad series I read a longtime ago about a man trying to sell a sewing machine. The ad in the newspaper ran like this:

Monday: FOR SALE—R.D. Jones has one sewing machine for sale. Phone 948–0707 after 7 p.m. and ask for Mrs. Kelly who lives with him cheap.

Tuesday: NOTICE—We regret having erred in R.D. Jones's ad yesterday. It should have read: One sewing machine for sale. Cheap. Phone 948–0707 and ask for Mrs. Kelly who lives with him after 7 p.m.

Wednesday: NOTICE—R.D. Jones has informed us that he has received several annoying telephone calls because of the error we made in his classified ad yesterday. His ad stands corrected as follows: FOR SALE—R.D. Jones has one sewing machine for sale. Cheap. Phone 948–0707 after 7 p.m. and ask for Mrs. Kelly who lives with him.

Thursday: NOTICE—I, R.D. Jones, have NO sewing machine for sale. I SMASHED IT. Don't call 948–0707, as the telephone has been disconnected. I have not been carrying on with Mrs. Kelly. Until yesterday she was my housekeeper, but she quit.[173]

Sometimes, no matter what you do, things just turn out bad. The world has a way of dealing us bad days. If you are anything like me, I get one bad day that turns into a week of bad days. Once they hit, they seem to keep hitting.

You'll have bad days on the journey to transformation. You'll want to quit. You'll ask yourself why you thought this program of change would be different. But here's the deal—bad feelings tend to outweigh good benefits. I know, it sounds counterintuitive. We say things like, "Good wins in the end." While this is true, getting to the end of any problem or self-improvement regimen is the hard part. This is why Paul encouraged the Galatians to stay steady and keep going. "Let us not become weary in doing good, for at the proper time we will reap a harvest if we do not give up" (Galatians 6:9). Why is it so hard to persevere?

THE NEGATIVITY BIAS

In the 1990s, psychologist Roy Baumeister studied what is now known as the *negativity effect*—which is the universal tendency for negative events and emotions to affect us more strongly than positive ones. For example, being devastated by a word of criticism outweighs a shower of praise. We dismiss 99 great and glorious comments and focus on the one bad comment. Bad can be stronger than good. In John Tierney and Roy F Baumeister's book, *The Power of Bad,* they say that we need four good days to offset one bad day. R.L. Jones had four straight days of bad. No wonder he smashed the sewing machine. But if you have four good days at work, Monday through Thursday, that's usually enough in a typical week to make up for a bad Friday. They call this the *rule of four*, which they say is a good way to think of any self-improvement regimen.

Tierney and Baumeister write:

> "People often abandon New Year's resolutions because they set unrealistic goals for themselves and then give up after the first slip. Dieters routinely succumb to what nutrition researchers call the what-the-hell effect: Now that I've broken the diet with that bowl of ice cream, I may as well finish off the carton. Instead of demanding perfection and despairing when you fail, you could aim to stick to your regimen at least four days out of five."[174]

NEGATIVITY EFFECT/NEGATIVITY BIAS
Things of a more negative nature (e.g. unpleasant thoughts, emotions, or social interactions; harmful/traumatic events) have a greater effect on one's psychological state than neutral or positive things.

RULE OF FOUR
It takes four good days to offset one bad day. Realistic goals aim for sticking to a regimen four days out of five so that the positive gains outweigh any negative setbacks.

The power of bad is *bad*. And bad likes to dominate the peak-end rule, as we've seen in the last chapter. Before I show you how to reset the peak-end rule, let's investigate why bad is more powerful than good.

Psychologists have known for years that we can be scarred by a single event of trauma. The emotional scar tissue never really goes away. We shove it down and do our best to cover it up with success, or wealth, or self-medicating to try and heal the hurt. I wouldn't ask you to tell your trauma blow-for-blow and relive it. But I think we must understand the power of bad when it's left to fester beneath our psyches. Pushing trauma into our Automatic Systems doesn't erase it. It takes on an unconscious life in a different form. It causes us to pay special attention to external threats and thus exaggerate those dangers, which is what happened to me after my car wreck. I feared death every time I got in a car. I refused to fly in a plane for many years. I did not like the feeling of being out of control.

Tierney and Baumeister write, "To figure out how well a person or a couple or a group is doing and to overcome the negativity bias, you need a method of weighing the positive against the negative to determine their relative strength. You need to ask: Just how bad is bad?"[175]

Evaluate in the situation, just how bad is this bad? I think we should reject the peak-end rule's initial result that life is bad and will never be the same again. If we believe there will never be a good day from this moment forward, then we are allowing the negativity bias to rule our thoughts and emotions. We are disqualifying the positive. So, why is bad so bad?

Bad is bad because the negativity bias erodes our existential meaning by making us addicted to safety. "We pay so much attention to bad things—reliving them, imagining them, avoiding them—that we let fear run our lives and become irrationally cautious. We are so focused on averting one obvious danger that we . . . pass up opportunities for happiness and success in our personal lives . . . "[176] And the subtle pitfall is to lose our purpose and meaning in life. An addiction to safety locks us in a fixed mindset and keeps us from growing.

However, it seems that we wake-up or take self-inventory at the end of each decade we live. The ending of a decade makes us question everything, even our identity. Take these 9-enders, for example.

9-ENDERS BECOME SELF-AWARE

Social psychologists Adam Alter and Hal Hershfield have studied a phenomenon they call "9-enders," which basically means that we audit our meaningfulness as we approach a new decade. "Six studies show that adults undertake a search for existential meaning when they approach a new decade in age (e.g., at ages 29, 39, 49, etc.) or imagine entering a new epoch, which leads them to behave in ways that suggest an ongoing or failed search for meaning (e.g., by exercising more vigorously, seeking extramarital affairs, or choosing to end their lives)."[177] Alter and Hershfield found that 9-enders are overrepresented among first-time marathoners by a whopping 48%.[178] Why? They are searching for new meaning. Something stronger than the power of bad. They want to feel alive again.

Endings make us question meaning and energize us to achieve it or to decline into hopelessness. This is why the peak-end rule is so dangerous—it robs us of meaning. Use this moment to disengage from the meaningless past. Make a fresh start. Part ways with your inferior self. Reimagine and reawake! Pay attention to the value of your life. Set some goals that have meaning to you. Changing the meaning of our lives creates new energy. It nudges our unconscious off autopilot. Renewing our minds is a process that takes self-awareness and effort. Remember what Stephen Covey writes, "Self-awareness enables us to stand apart and examine even the way we 'see' ourselves—our self-paradigm, the most fundamental paradigm of effectiveness."[179]

If we know the peak-end rule is our memory of a situation dominated by the negative outcome (disqualifying the positive), then we will now need at least four good memories to counteract the bad memory. Tomorrow we will take some further steps toward resetting the peak-end rule. Today let's focus on how we can take advantage of the rule of four.

REFLECTIONS:

1. John Tierney and Roy F Baumeister say we need four good days to offset one bad day. How many bad days have you had this week? How many were good?

2. Did the good days offset the bad? Why or why not?

3. How can you end today on a good note?

4. R.D. Jones smashed his sewing machine. Got anything you want to smash? What's holding you back from smashing something and freeing yourself from it?

NOSTALGIA: LOOKING BACK TO MOVE FORWARD

Nostalgia isn't what it used to be.

—PETER DE VRIES

One of my favorite Twilight Zone episodes is about a middle-aged businessman named Martin. He works in a big suburban city where it's a dog-eat-dog business environment. He's fighting to stay alive inside brutal competition. One day, he gets in his car and starts driving until he comes upon a small town. He stops and starts walking around the town, realizing he's in his childhood hometown. Suddenly, he realizes he's back in time. Everything is exactly as it was when he was ten years old. He even runs into himself as a boy and he calls out for ten-year-old Martin to stop so he can talk to himself as a boy. Next, he goes to his old house and tries to tell his father who he is and that he has traveled back in time to be his father's little boy again.

This is one of my favorite episodes because when I was struggling through a recent dark night of the soul, I longed to go all the way back to childhood—back before the car wreck—and start over. Just like Martin. I knew I'd change things by making different choices. But who was I kidding? That only happens in the Twilight Zone. We can change the way we remember an experience, but not the choices we made. This reality creates most of the pain.

THE DREAM

For about 25 years, I had this recurring dream of being back at my junior high school—Medina Junior High. It was probably the most joyful period of my life. I played games in the neighborhood with my friends and our bikes took us everywhere. It was a time of innocence and play. My favorite thing was playing basketball with Doug, Ron, Jimmy, and Fred. The world was opening up for us and I had all these great dreams of what I was going to do with my life and what I was going to be. Everything seemed possible. Our mindsets were only growth. Life was before us. It was just beginning. For years, I would wake up in the middle of this dream of being back in junior high; longing to go back the way Martin in the Twilight Zone longed to go back. In my dream, I was on the outside of the junior high school and all the doors were locked and I couldn't get in. I would go around the gym and look in the windows, longing to get inside. I would wake up from the dream and feel an incredible sadness and longing. I dreamed this over and over for years and years. It would haunt me and make me long for a time when everything was possible. I even wanted to sleep, just so I could have that dream.

I get emotional now just thinking about dreaming that dream over and over. Longing and thirsting to go back, just like Martin. I wanted to find the twelve-year-old boy and tell him not to waste his possibility and to soar at the mountaintops. But I have had an epiphany about nostalgia. I discovered what that dream was trying to tell me, which led me to a revelation about nostalgia that is backed up by research. Nostalgia can help us rediscover the positive things in our past that the remembering self has disqualified. Nostalgia can reset the peak-end rule and create a paradigm shift. Let me show you how it works, but first a little history on nostalgia.

ORIGINS OF NOSTALGIA

Nostalgia was coined in a seventeenth-century Swiss medical dissertation to identify a neurological disease of essentially demonic cause. The medical student, Johannes Hofer, combined the Greek words for homecoming (nostos) and pain (algos) to describe the homesickness observed in Swiss mercenary soldiers fighting abroad. Nostalgia was so debilitating that Swiss officers banned, under penalty of death, the playing of an Alpine milking song that supposedly triggered the disease. Must have been a powerful song! But just think of songs you know from your high school days.

NOSTALGIA
A sentimental longing or wistful affection for the past, typically for a period or place with happy personal associations.

By the beginning of the 20th century, nostalgia was regarded as a psychiatric disorder. Symptoms included anxiety, sadness, and insomnia. By the mid-20th century, psychodynamic approaches considered nostalgia a subconscious desire to return to an earlier life stage and it was labeled as a repressive compulsive disorder. Then it was downgraded to a variant of depression, marked by loss and grief, though still equated with homesickness. By the late 20th century, nostalgia and homesickness parted ways. Homesickness studies focused on separation anxiety. On the other hand, nostalgia has become known as a "sentimental longing for one's past."[180] I read in a psychology research paper, "Nostalgia has a long past and an exciting future."[181] I thought, "Really? Nostalgia?"

According to Dr. Clay Routledge, Social Psychologist and Associate Professor of Psychology at North Dakota State University, nostalgia "increases positive mood, self-esteem, feelings of social connectedness, optimism about the future, and perceptions of meaning in life. Furthermore, nostalgia motivates people to focus on cultivating meaningful relationships and pursue important life goals. In addition, as people get older, nostalgia makes them feel youthful and energetic. Nostalgia also reduces existential fears about death."[182]

In one study, British and American undergraduates wrote narratives about a "nostalgic event" (vs. an "ordinary event") in their lives and reflected briefly upon the event and how it made them feel. Researchers discovered that the simultaneous expression of happiness and sadness was more common in narratives of nostalgic events than in ordinary events. Positive ordinary events rarely gave rise to both happiness and sadness, but this coactivation of happiness and sadness occurred frequently following the recollection of a nostalgic event. Even so, nostalgic memories created more happiness than sadness.[183] What does all this mean to us in our study together?

Let me start by saying that nostalgia can quickly become regret if we are not careful. It can erode a sense of meaning in the present. If we are fixated on better days gone by, then we will not reap the benefits of nostalgia. Finding meaning is important to any form of remembering our past. We are not pushing for an existential crisis, but a coactivation of happiness and sadness that can create a paradigm shift.

When we spend some time thinking about and journaling about nostalgic events, it helps us lay down richer memories that can change the peak-end rule. This is one of the main goals of a paradigm shift—seeing everything with new eyes. The old narrative must not be eliminated—it needs to be reconstructed by editing the "video" memory clips and rearranging them in a coherent cinema-like story. Nostalgia is one way the brain edits and arranges the images. Think of it as a looking back while looking forward. How do we want our stories to end?

Let's go back to David and his nostalgia for a drink of water from a well in his boyhood Bethlehem. Was it wrong for him to desire it? No as researchers have discovered, nostalgizing is a good thing. The nostagia turned into a bad thing when his men tried to fulfill the longing. I think nostalgia may be bad for us if we go to extremes to reproduce the past. But reliving the past in memories is a healing thing. John Tierney and Roy F. Baumeister write, in their book, *The Power of Bad,* "Nostalgia isn't a purely positive emotion. It's bittersweet, tinged with a sense of loss, but it's ultimately rewarding."[184] This is the healing aspect of nostalgia—it produces a bittersweet reward. It is not pie-in-the-sky or a sense of total failure. It's reality for the brain. It says to the peak-end rule, "Yes, some things have been bad, but what about these things?" And it points out the positive without totally erasing the negative past. It offers us a tipping point—that sweet spot in between where a small change makes a big difference. It gives us the balance we lack. It neutralizes the drain of negativity.

David's nostalgia may have been his way of healing the quagmire of battle; and good should have been left alone instead of his men getting involved and trying to recreate the past. So, I'm not in favor of recreating the past, but participating in nostalgic memories to change the peak-end rule is beneficial.

RICHER MEMORIES

There was once a couple that had been married for 60 years. They were sitting on the front porch together feeling romantic. The wife said, "I remember when you used to always hold my hand."

Her husband reached over and took her hand.

She said, "I remember when you always used to kiss me on the cheek."

He leaned over and kissed her on the cheek.

She said, "I even remember when you used to nibble on my ear."

He got up and started walking away.

She said, "What's wrong? Where are you going?"

He turned around and said, "I'm going to get my teeth."

"Memories are all we get to keep from our experience of living and the only perspective that we can adopt as we think about our lives is therefore that of the remembering self."[185] So it comes down to arranging these memories to tell a coherent story all the way to the end of our lives—teeth and no teeth. "By so doing, nostalgia can help one navigate successfully the vicissitudes of daily life."[186]

Nostalgia is positive and negative, because today may never be as wonderful as the good, old days. Things tend to never be what they used to be. And the man could have bemoaned not having teeth to nibble with or he could accept reality and go get his teeth. At least he didn't disqualify the positive and wish for good, old days only. He lived in the moment with the tinge of bittersweet nostalgia.

Make the best of the life you have by remembering a nostalgic event today. In the reflection questions, you'll be given an opportunity to journal about such an event.

REFLECTION

1. Journal about a "nostalgic event," and then list below the positive parts and the negative parts of your nostalgic memory:

   Positive thoughts:

   Negative thoughts:

2. How could you change the negative peak-end rule into a positive memory?

SMALL WINS

Little by little one walks far.

—PERUVIAN PROVERB

The school system in a large city had a program to help children keep up with their schoolwork during stays in the city's hospitals. One day a teacher who was assigned to the program received a routine call asking her to visit a particular child. She took the child's name and room number and talked briefly with the child's regular class teacher. "We're studying nouns and adverbs in his class now," the regular teacher said, "and I'd be grateful if you could help him, so he doesn't fall too far behind."

The hospital program teacher went to see the boy that afternoon. No one had mentioned to her that the boy had been badly burned and was in great pain. Upset at the sight of the boy, she stammered as she told him, "I've been sent by your school to help you with nouns and adverbs." When she left his room after working with him, she felt she hadn't accomplished much.

But the next day, a nurse asked her, "What did you do to that boy?"

The teacher felt she must have done something wrong and began to apologize.

"No, no," said the nurse. "You don't know what I mean. We've been worried about that little boy, but ever since yesterday, his whole attitude has changed. He's fighting back, responding to treatment. It's as though he's decided to live."

When the teacher asked the boy to explain why his attitude had improved, he told her that he had completely given up hope until she arrived to teach him nouns and adverbs. Everything changed when he came to a simple realization. He expressed it this way: "They wouldn't send a teacher to work on nouns and adverbs with a dying boy, would they?"[187]

This is what I'd call a small win in the realm of perspective. When I feel isolated and disconnected—filled with despair—this is my fixed mindset. And my narrative is a result of this mindset. I feel unlovable and helpless. When we sense no hope, we miss possible new outcomes. But hope keeps us alive to possibility. This is why working on a process to change is important every day. We need small wins. The boy didn't see the big picture of healing, only a small piece of it. But he had hope in the midst of circumstances that hadn't changed. His hope came from his positive perspective and this hope produced a willingness to change. It created the growth mindset. "To survive, life has to win every day. Death has to win just once."[188]

Having small wins will be critical as you transform your mindset. James Clear writes:

> "Too often, we convince ourselves that massive success requires massive action . . . Meanwhile, improving by 1% isn't particularly notable—sometimes it isn't even noticeable—but it can be far more meaningful, especially in the long run. The difference a tiny improvement can make over time is astounding. Here's how the math works out: if you can get 1% better each day for one year, you'll end up thirty-seven times better by the time you're done."[189]

One Cornell professor wrote in 1984, "Small wins are a steady application of a small advantage. Once a small win has been accomplished, forces are set in motion that favor another small win." It convinces people that bigger achievements are within reach.[190]

In research on creative work done by Teresa M. Amabile and Steven J. Kramer, they discovered what they call the *progress principle*. "Of all the things that can boost emotions, motivation, and perceptions during a workday, the single most important is making progress in meaningful work. And the more frequently people experience that sense of progress, the more likely they are to be creatively productive in the long run."[191] A small win can make all the difference in how we feel and perform. They analyzed 12,000 diary entries of employees from a variety of industries and found that 76% of people reported that their best days involved making progress toward goals.[192] So focus on progress and you'll have a great day. But research also shows that a setback has between two and five times as much emotional impact as a positive event. Emotions make us less rational and therefore more susceptible to the power of a setback.[193]

PROGRESS PRINCIPLE
Making progress in meaningful work boosts your emotions, motivation and perceptions.

Not only are small wins vital for motivation, but small wins are the only way our brains transform. Plasticity—the process of change in the brain—only occurs in small spots in the brain. The first reason is because practiced pathways become difficult to exit. The upside is a lightning-fast brain that makes solving problems easier. The downside is that older brains are less flexible. Change can occur, but only in small spots, as steered by relevance. In contrast, a baby's brain changes across a vast expanse in their brain. As we've learned, relevance creates more territory in the brain. The North Star of plasticity is relevance.[194]

We can all produce small wins. Too many times we want sudden success, or we want God to reveal the whole plan. We want to see the future—the full picture. But most often God deals with us in small ways. We only need to trust His ways.

The following story will illustrate how to focus on small wins when we cannot see the full picture.

PLANK-BY-PLANK

A young woman was on her way to China where she would serve as missionary, teaching in a Christian school. She had to travel by boat and she found the voyage to be long and difficult. She had many concerns about this and wondered how she would be able to survive the journey. One night, she had a dream in which she was standing on a plank out in the ocean. In her dream, God told her to start walking toward China. She said she could not do it. She could not walk on water. But the voice insisted, so she stepped out to the end of the plank and another plank appeared. Each time she reached the end of one plank, another was there. When she woke up, she accepted this dream as a promise from God. She would be able to follow one promise at a time, one plank at a time, until she fulfilled her dream of being a missionary.

Be mindful of looking for just one plank. Take the step. Don't look back. Whatever happened yesterday, whatever mistakes were made, whatever slips and struggles, victories, good things—all of yesterday— no longer matters. It's all in the past. Also, don't worry about tomorrow because there's no guarantee that tomorrow will even come. All you have is today. Focus on today. Remain present. Stay on the path today. The path that you stay on every day that will lead you to your destination. What am I going to do today to meet my goals? Follow your North star or your exemplary cause—Jesus—let Him guide you today. Pay attention. Know where you are. Know where you're going. Know how you're going to get there. Be mindful of the new neural pathways you are cocreating with God. Cocreation is key for a new mindset.

REFLECTIONS

1. *Fast Company* magazine cofounder, Alan Webber, offers a simple exercise for assessing whether we're on a mission with purpose or not. Get a few blank three-by-five-inch cards. On one of the cards, write your answer to this question: "What gets you up in the morning?" Now, on the other side of the card, write your answer to another question: "What keeps you up at night?" "If you don't like an answer, toss the card and try again until you've crafted something you can live with. Then read what you've produced. If both answers give you a sense of meaning and direction . . . use them as your compass."[195]

2. What is one small thing you can do today to make progress toward change?

DESTINATION POSTCARDS

*. . . But hope that is seen is no hope at all.
Who hopes for what they already have? But if we hope for
what we do not yet have, we wait for it patiently.*

—ROMANS 8:24-25

When the army of the king of Babylon was sweeping down on Jerusalem (Jeremiah 32), Hanamel, Jeremiah's cousin sold Jeremiah a piece of property for fourteen dollars that was being camped on by the invading army. It was a worthless piece of land at that point. It'd be a lot like Scarlett O'Hara selling her family homestead, Tara,—house and all—when she sees the Yankees marching into Atlanta. It would be like Scarlett O'Hara saying to herself, "Scarlett, the Yankees are coming and you've got to sell Tara before they burn it to the ground." How many of us would have purchased her house and land?

Before Hanamel offered to sell his land to Jeremiah, God came to Jeremiah and told him to buy the field. He told Jeremiah, "For the LORD Almighty, the God of Israel, says: 'Someday people will again own property here in this land and will buy and sell houses and vineyards and fields'" (Jeremiah 32:15).

How many of us would have bet our souls against history and bought that field? Jeremiah stood there in the doubt of the moment, right before the invading army swept through to ransack and blister Jerusalem, thinking, "God said that one day this field will prosper."

Anyone can say, "Sure, it's possible. The field could fall back into Jeremiah's possession. But what are the odds? Once the Babylonians takeover, all bets are off." But what did God say?

Bible commentators believe buying that field was a deliberate act of hope. Eugene Peterson writes, "Hope commits us to actions that connect with God's promises."[196] This is why vision is so important to creating the life we've always wanted. We must create what researchers Chip and Dan Heath call *destination postcards.* [197] A destination postcard is a vivid picture from the near-term future that shows what's possible. Jeremiah was given a destination postcard when God told him that someday people will again own property here in this land and will buy and sell houses and vineyards and fields. This destination postcard created hope and internalized his participation with God. It gave him a vision of what God was going to do in the near-term future. This destination postcard was a promise from God.

To create the life we've always wanted, we must create destination postcards. We must envision what we want to become, despite the odds that are against us. Jeremiah was choosing a different future potential by hoping, anticipating, and expecting a different result—the land would one day be redeemed. Dispenza writes, "In other words, if you mentally rehearse that unknown future with a clear intention and an elevated emotion and do it repeatedly, then . . . you should have real neuroplastic changes in your brain and epigenetic changes in your body."[198]

DESTINATION POSTCARD
A vivid picture from the near-term future that shows what could be possible.

Hope activates God's promises and these promises change the wiring in our brain. We are buying into what we believe, which places our hope in the future result of God's promises. Our minds work together with God's promises by eliminating the external environment of hopelessness and then the future no longer looks bleak. Instead, we mentally rehearse God's promises.

Not trusting in God's promises, the ego is disconnected from God's reality and keeps us in the mode of trying to predict the future on our own, which always leads to disintegration within. The ego protects itself with a toxic belief and anytime we want to change our mindset, it reminds us that nothing can change. The one thing the ego fears is change, so we disengage to protect our ego.

When we trust God's promises, we participate in the divine nature, which infuses us with energy. We gain our strength by this participation. Isn't this what God intended when he had Jeremiah buy that field? Peterson writes, "All acts of hope expose themselves to ridicule because they seem impractical, failing to conform to visible reality. But in fact they are the reality that is being constructed but is not yet visible."[199] Therefore, thought alone creates this divine participation. We have the mind of Christ. When our mind visualizes God's promises, it produces a destination postcard that lives in the future hope of God's reality.

We must do something in the present that allows us to participate in the future with God. We open our minds to the unseen. No doubt Jeremiah visualized his field with houses and vineyards being built once again. This is the only way we hope. He walked by faith and not by sight.

Hope is an act of visualization. Dispenza writes, "When you're truly focused on an intention for some future outcome, if you can make inner thought more real than the outer environment during the process, the brain won't know the difference between the two. Then your body, as the unconscious mind, will begin to experience the new future event in the present moment. You'll signal new genes, in new ways, to prepare for this imagined future event."[200] The brain is training the Automatic System how to act automatically in the future. As we've seen: thoughts are powerful. When these thoughts become new habits, we're transformed.

We must be confident of what we hope for and have assurance about what we do not see (Hebrews 11:1). Jeremiah knew God was working in the unseen world and redeeming his field so that it would come back in a new form. It is a picture of what happens to us when we put on the new self. Scripture even says, "For we are co-workers in God's service; you are God's field, God's building" (1 Corinthians 3:9). Planting thoughts in God's field raises a crop of security and peace reframing old destructive thoughts.

Awareness of the Divine's presence—already working in the world—is true awakening. Jeremiah knew how to awaken his soul and foster hope in God's future. Having the mind of Christ—who is the true vine and we are its branches. If we abide in Him, then we rise above our environment by rehearsing God's promises in our minds. These thoughts lead us to the proper action between stimulus and response. This is where real transformation occurs. Between stimulus and response, you must do something in that space that allows you to participate in the future with God. In this space, think on things above.

Start each day by planting thoughts in God's field—one day at a time, until you grow a new crop. Weed out the toxic thoughts by asking: "Are these thoughts moving me closer to becoming the person I've always wanted to be?" Between stimulus and response input a positive thought.

REFLECTIONS

1. Create a seed bag for new seed thoughts that will become your
   new crop. Take a brown paper bag or shoebox for the seed bag.
   On a sheet of paper, write down one positive word a day. Think on
   each word for five minutes, then place it inside the seed bag. Do
   this for the next 14 days. Whenever you have a negative thought,
   think on this daily positive thought. This will create mindfulness.
   Until we capture our negative thoughts and replace them, our
   thoughts won't change.

2. Take a 3x5 index card and write down your destination postcard,
   which is the life you've always wanted that you are cocreating
   with God.

3. Connect your destination postcard to one of God's promises. Write the promise on your index card. Below are just a few of the 7,500 promises in the Bible:

I will never leave you or forsake you.

—HEBREWS 13:5

No one will snatch you out of my hand.

—JOHN 10:28

I know the plans I have for you. To give you a hope and a future.

—JEREMIAH 29:11

So do not fear, for I am with you, do not be dismayed,
for I am your God. I will strengthen you and help you;
I will uphold you with my righteous right hand.

—ISAIAH 41:10

BELIEF AND EXPECTATION

*I'm such an optimist I'd go after Moby Dick in a rowboat
and take the tartar sauce with me.*

—ZIG ZIGLAR

The parents of twin boys—one an incurable optimist and one an incurable pessimist—were worried about the extremes of their behavior and attitudes, so they took the boys to see a psychologist. The psychologist observed them for a while and then said that they could be easily helped. He put the pessimist in a room filled with all the toys a boy could want, which would allow him to enjoy life. He put the optimist in another room filled with horse manure. Then they observed both boys through one-way mirrors. The pessimist continued to be a pessimist, stating that he had no one to play with. But when they went to look in on the optimist, they were astounded to find him digging through the manure. The psychologist ran into the room and asked what on earth the boy was doing. The boy said, "With all this manure, there has to be a pony in here somewhere."

Belief and expectancy may not produce a pony, but studies have proven that belief and expectancy have enormous impacts on the brain. Studies on the placebo effect have affirmed this. Belief and expectancy are key elements in the placebo effect and in hope. Placebos depend on belief and expectancy, so we should give them a second look in the realm of transformation and see how they work.

Dr. Jerome Groopman believes pain amplifies our sense of hopelessness. He goes on to say that when we feel pain from our physical debility, that pain amplifies our sense of hopelessness, because the less hopeful we feel, the fewer endorphins and enkephalins we release and the more cholecystokinin, or CCK, we release. CCK works in part by blocking endorphins and enhancing pain. The more pain we experience due to CCK, the less able we are to feel hope. He says to break this cycle we need a spark of hope, which tempers pain.[201] But where does this spark of hope come from? It comes from belief and expectation.

For a placebo to work, a person must believe and expect he is getting the real drug, thereby releasing endorphins and enkephalins which create hope. Hope helps us overcome the hurdle of pain that keeps us from moving forward. How does this happen? We must believe we have real choices.

It goes back to the pause between stimulus and response. "Hope is linked to a sense of control, both over oneself and over external forces . . ."[202] Before you make a response to your circumstances, you must believe and expect that you can overcome. Why try otherwise? What holds us back from moving forward is pain. We experience pain and stop creating the life we've always wanted. Then our subsequent toxic beliefs are the result of the pain of our past experience. Dr. Dispenza writes, "So the only way to change your beliefs and perceptions in order to create a placebo response is to change your state of being. You have to finally see your old, limiting beliefs for what they are—records of the past—and be willing to let go of them so that you can embrace new beliefs about yourself that will help you create a new future."[203]

We need a belief to live from and a dream to live for. The fixed mindset rooted in past experiences must go. Our growth mindset must express a future you haven't fully imagined, but you still long for. To change your paradigm, you will need to rewrite your narrative the way the jilted bride did in Day 1. The dream you live for is what is written on your destination postcard you created in Day 23. Now you must believe and expect God's help. Dr. Groopman writes, "Instilling hope in the brain involves setting a firm goal and anticipating the reward of living with the dream fulfilled."[204]

Hope is the spark that will change your state of being. It's the result of endorphins and enkephalins firing in the brain. Hope is a chemical reaction that looks beyond adversity to a desired future event that generates a different vision of your condition.[205] Hope is all about what you believe in and what you are expecting. Once you dream up a new life, you must envision it—sparking the release of endorphins and enkephalins. The placebo effect works in a same way. Hope is sparked and your brain is flooded with endorphins and enkephalins.

YOUR EXPLANATORY STYLE

One of the easiest ways to gain a mindset of growth is by using what Martin Seligman calls an *explanatory style*. Seligman writes, "Explanatory style is the manner in which you habitually explain to yourself why events happen."[206] He believes each of us carries a word in his or her heart—a "no" or a "yes." When we carry a "no," then we believe the bad events in our life are permanent. We believe there is no possibility of change—"whatever I do doesn't matter"—which creates the quitting response. When we carry a "yes," then we believe bad events are temporary. They can be overcome. We can change and transform.

EXPLANATORY STYLE
How one explains to themself why they experience a particular event as either positive or negative.

People with a "no" will give up easily and believe the causes of the bad events will always be there to affect their lives. Viktor Frankl, a WWII concentration camp survivor, calls this *provisional existence.* He says that the prisoners in the concentration camp lived in a provisional existence of unknown limit, because they did not know when their suffering would end. They weren't sure they'd ever be freed from the camps. They could not plan ahead, so the prisoners found themselves unable to cope with their situations. He said many of them would quit eating, or wouldn't get out of bed. As a result, their immune systems just shut down and they got sick and died. All because they didn't have anything to live for. They were hopeless. They had nothing to put their hope in, so they didn't see any reason to live. They believed the bad events were permanent. This is how we place a "no" in our heart and believe change is not possible.

PROVISIONAL EXISTENCE
Life has lost purpose, focus and hope such that one cannot plan for any conceivable future.

When we replace the "no" with a "yes" in our hearts, then we have made a paradigm shift. This is how we turn bad events into only temporary setbacks. We move with the pain into the realm of possibility by telling ourselves, "I am relentless. I will persevere. Something will change. God is with me." It puts a "yes" in your heart.

REFLECTIONS

1. Do you believe bad events are permanent?

2. Do you have a "yes" or a "no" in your heart?

LETTING GO OF YOUR ATTACHMENTS

So (the prodigal son) went and hired himself out to a citizen
of that country, who sent him to his fields to feed pigs.
He longed to fill his stomach with the pods that the pigs
were eating, but no one gave him anything.

When he came to his senses, he said, "How many of my father's
hired servants have food to spare, and here I am starving to death!
I will set out and go back to my father and say to him:
Father, I have sinned against heaven and against you.
I am no longer worthy to be called your son; make me like
one of your hired servants." So he got up and went to his father.

—LUKE 15:15–20

In *Journey to Freedom*, I wrote about a television program that showed a method for trapping monkeys. The natives made a hole in a log and put bait of fruit inside. The hole was just big enough to allow a monkey room to get his opened hand inside the log. The monkey reached his hand in to get the fruit, but when his fingers closed around it, he couldn't fit his fist back through the hole. The monkey was determined to hang on to the fruit and soon he was captured—trapped by something he refused to detach from. Crazy, right? Because he's only trapped by his desire for the fruit. He's not physically trapped. He only needs to open his hand and run, but he hangs on to the fruit—to his own detriment. He's trapped by his own paradigm. He sees what he wants to see. He misses the new pattern that has emerged. His hand is caught by a belief—they are trying to get my fruit.

Like monkeys, we hang on to things that are detrimental to our souls, unwilling to let go because we feel we are in control. We see what we want to see until it's too late.

The bond between human and vice is called an attachment. Gerald May writes, "Addiction sidetracks and eclipses the energy of our deepest, truest desire for love and goodness. We succumb because the energy of our desire becomes attached or shall we say nailed to specific behaviors, objects, or people. Attachment, then, is the process that enslaves desire and creates the state of addiction."[207] And these "objects of attachment then become preoccupations and obsessions; they come to rule our lives."[208]

ATTACHMENT

Energy of our desire becomes attached to specific behaviors, objects, or people; the process that enslaves desire and creates the state of addiction

---

Attachments are those things we cling to for security, whether it be money, self-image, a career status, an addiction, any dysfunctional relationship, maintaining an outrageous lifestyle, or any other unwanted vice that takes the place of God. We fiercely cling to them because we believe they offer security or status, even if it's false security. When circumstances force us to either let go or hang on to our attachment, we ask:

How will I cope without my vice (addiction)?

How will I live without this relationship?

How can I risk losing what's keeping me alive?

How can I tell my child no and risk losing my child's love?

If people really knew the truth about me, they'd stop loving me. So, I must keep the lie going.

The thought of losing our attachments terrifies us—even when they are dysfunctional and destructive. The prodigal son had his attachments. He enslaved himself—after squandering his inheritance—by making the wrong attachment. "He went and joined himself to a citizen of that country; and (the citizen) sent him into his fields to feed swine" (Luke 15:15, KJV). Notice that he *joined* himself. The Greek word is *kollaó,* meaning "to glue, unite." He attached himself—glued himself—to someone he thought would get him out of despair, but feeding pigs was a violation of his Jewish heritage. A Jewish boy would never get involved with pigs. His attachment to the man led to the loss of his Jewish dignity. He could've returned home to the father and discovered unconditional love. But he chose to go further away from the source of love.

Detaching from an attachment causes anxiety, because we are letting go of the illusion of security and control. This is scary for most of us. "What will I become without it?" This fear keeps us in bondage. Most of us never get beyond this place of anxiety to truly transform our lives because we can't let go of control—even when it's killing us. We really believe our own lie that we are in control. We use our attachments to bury our feelings of shame and guilt, so we can hide from the truth about our human condition.

Feeling anxiety and wanting to run from vulnerability when someone wants to get to know us on a deeper level is how we know the ego is still in control .

Dr. Joe Dispenza writes, "Your past shortfalls can be traced, at their root, to one major oversight: you haven't committed yourself to living by the truth that **your thoughts have consequences so great that they create your reality.**"[209] What was the monkey's reality? He thought the fruit belonged to him and that the natives were after the fruit— this thought had dire consequences. His unwillingness to change his thoughts fostered his attachment and his entrapment. He only needed to let go.

LETTING GO

So how do we let go of our attachments? We have to allow ourselves to be fully known. No more secrets. We become vulnerable. This is why I'm disclosing my pain and failure to you in this book. I must remain open and vulnerable to disintegrate the ego's power and remain free of the "me first" trap. Only vulnerability deals the final blow to our ego and as Brené Brown writes, "When we pretend that we can avoid vulnerability, we engage in behaviors that are often inconsistent with who we want to be. Experiencing vulnerability isn't a choice—the only choice we have is how we're going to respond when we are confronted with uncertainty, risk, and emotional exposure."[210]

To truly transform we must be known. We must stop pretending and come out of hiding. Curt Thompson writes,

> "If you allow yourself to be known by God, you invite a different and frankly more terrifying experience. You are now in a position of vulnerability. If you permit others to know you, they can make their own assessment of your worth. They can react to you. You give them the power to be affected by you and in so doing to affect you. You grant them the option to love you or to reject you. In essence, you must—must trust another with yourself.

> However, I will argue that it is only through this process of being known that you come to know yourself and learn how to know others. There is no other way. To be known is to be pursued, examined, and shaken. To be known is to be loved and to have hopes and even demands placed on you . . . To be known means that you allow your shame and guilt to be exposed—in order for them to be healed."[211]

Unless we are willing to be known, nothing changes. The ego is still in control in the shadows of our minds, running the automatic unconscious program, conforming us to the patterns of this world, making us work for conditional love, telling us we must be better, do better, climb higher in the ranks of the world. More power, more fame, more wealth, more accolades. We build this tough exterior of having it all together when inside we are falling apart. Only vulnerability loosens our attachment's stranglehold.

We must feel secure in God's love to move into a place of vulnerability. Until we make a secure attachment with God, we will never fully let go of the old life we hate. We have to hear God say, "I am enough, so you will be enough."

So don't run from vulnerability. For in running, you may become involved—as the prodigal son did—in behaviors that are often inconsistent with who you want to be. This is always the danger. With inconsistent behavior, we lose our dignity; we lose our true selves. So let go of your attachments. Don't keep holding on like the monkey to an idea that is trapping you. It's only a fixed mindset. Let go!

REFLECTIONS

1. Name the one thing that makes you feel secure. Is it wealth, beauty, status, etc.?

2. What emotion do you feel when you think about vulnerability and being known?

3. How can you let go of an unhealthy attachment?

REBUILDING OUR STORY

TOXIC SHAME AS AN IDENTITY

So I find this law at work: Although I want to do good,
evil is right there with me. For in my inner being
I delight in God's law; but I see another law at work in me,
waging war against the law of my mind and making me
a prisoner of the law of sin at work within me.
What a wretched man I am!

—ROMANS 7:21–4

Two men stand staring in front of a painting in an art gallery. In the painting, a man is playing chess with the devil. The devil is grinning ear-to-ear because he has the man cornered. The title of the painting, "Checkmate," indicates that the game is over. The devil has won. His opponent has failed. He has no more moves.

The first man looking at the painting wants to move on to view other paintings in the gallery. But the second man, an international chess champion, wants to look at the painting longer, so he waves his friend on and tells him he will catch up later. The chess champion stares and stares at the chessboard, then suddenly he steps back, flabbergasted. "It's wrong!" he exclaims. "There's one more move." He runs to his friend and together they look at the painting. "We have to contact the painter," the chess champion says. "It's not a checkmate. The man has one more move!"

Throughout the Bible, this game has been played—the Israelites found momentary freedom only to then face the formidable Red Sea with Pharaoh and his armies in hot pursuit. But the God had one more move!

Shame locks us in a psychological paralysis. But there's always one more move—and shame will offer us a way out. Curt Thompson writes, "Shame wants to alter our stories by telling its own version, one that is sure to bring trouble wherever it goes."[212]

The underbelly of the false self is shame. And when our identity is one of shame, we hide and cover-up our inadequacies, which in turn stunts growth. We don't feel like we have one more move. Then shame offers us one. Again, think of the prodigal son. He hit rock bottom in the pigpen and sought crisis-stabilization. He wanted a way out of the pigpen and shame had one more move. Shame told him that being a hired servant was the one move left available to him. Shame said, "Here's your script—you will never have your father's respect and be part of the family again, but at least as a hired servant you will have food to eat and won't look like a failure on this pig farm."

Once shame takes control of our lives, it creates a false self as a husk to protect our fragile ego. This is why a false self feels good and hopeful at first. It offers us a way out of the psychological pain of feeling like a failure. Richard Rohr writes, "Your false self, which we might also call your 'small self,' is your launching pad: your body image, your job, your education, your clothes, your money, your car, your sexual identity, your success, and so on."[213]

Creating a false self is how we look good to others in order to feel good about ourselves. It's just a layer of protection for the fragile ego. John Bradshaw writes, "(Toxic shame) divides us from ourselves and from others. When our feeling of shame becomes toxic shame, we disown ourselves. And this disowning demands a cover-up. Toxic shame parades in many garbs and get-ups."[214] The prodigal son's garb was being a hired servant, which was better than being a bankrupt, starving and filthy pig farmer.

SHAME
Feeling in response to wrongdoing or thinking something you believe is immoral. "I've done something wrong."

TOXIC SHAME
A chronic feeling of worthlessness. I am wrong.

Shame creates an inner paradigm of guilt and condemnation that causes us to disown ourselves, which creates the false self and we then get our identity from our body image, our job, our education, our clothes, our money, our car, our sexual identity, our success, or whatever. Then to quench the shame of feeling inadequate, we reach for attachments to help us further the lie that has become like a millstone around our necks. Like the apostle Paul in Romans 7, our true self wants to do what is right, but the false self is there demanding we look good for others to perpetuate the lie and protect the fragile ego.

I see so many people struggling with shame. Many have died spiritually in the wilderness of toxic shame by disowning themselves. It's systemic in our world, especially in American society. Social media feeds our failures and scandals and shortcomings. It's brutal. We're labeled smart or dumb, good or bad, pretty or ugly, rich or poor. Shame is dualistic. It says, "You're this or you're not that." We stop dreaming of who we can be and where we can go.

When God stirs up within us a vision of what we can become, shame will tell us why it's not possible. Shame wants to remain in control. But if we move against shame's lie, grace is there to rescue us from this wilderness. Thompson says we should shift "our attention from shame—and the story it is trying to tell—(and) back to the story that is true, the story that God is telling at this very moment. To scorn or disregard shame is to acknowledge it and turn away, as if we think nothing of it."[215]

The father welcomed the prodigal son home, back into the relationship as a son. Once grace was offered, the prodigal son stopped pursuing the position of being a hired servant. This is why grace is the most powerful agent of change in the universe. It demolishes the shame-based toxic autopilot self and reestablishes our authentic, true self as beloved children of God. Grace makes us into what we can never be on our own. Grace cocreates with us a new destiny with God. We allow ourselves to be more than shame's lie.

A.W. Tozer once wrote, "When God forgives (someone), he doesn't think, 'I will have to watch this (person) because they have a bad record.' No, he starts with the person again as though he had just been created and as if there had been no past at all."[216] This is the power of grace. It makes a new beginning possible. It doesn't condemn us or demand that we work our way back into right standing with God. It's a do-over with no strings attached.

Let's end today by naming and taming our shame.

REFLECTIONS

1. Richard Rohr explains a false self like this, "Your False Self, which we might also call your 'small self,' is your launching pad: your body image, your job, your education, your clothes, your money, your car, your sexual identity, your success, and so on." Have you formed a false self?

2. What is your false self covering up?

3. What is your most common shame story? How can you shift the
   shame story from "checkmate" to access "one more move" today?

THE IDEALIZED IMAGE

There is perhaps no one of our natural passions
so hard to subdue as pride. Beat it down, stifle it,
mortify it as much as one pleases, it is still alive.
Even if I could conceive that I had completely overcome it,
I should probably be proud of my humility.

—BENJAMIN FRANKLIN

A young woman asked for an appointment with her pastor to talk with him about a besetting sin that worried her. When she saw him, she said, "Pastor, I have become aware of a sin in my life which I cannot control. Every time I am at church I begin to look around at the other women and I realize that I am the prettiest one in the whole congregation. None of the others can compare with my beauty. What can I do about this sin?" The pastor replied, "Mary, that's not a sin, why that's just a mistake!"

We laugh, but we know people who think highly of themselves. Maybe it's warranted. Maybe they are more superior than everyone else. But the truth is we all have some aspect of what's called the idealized image.[217]

The idealized image is an inflated ego that flatters us with unmatched beauty, power, intelligence, saintliness, honesty, fame, etc. It makes us arrogant, which means to arrogate to oneself qualities that one does not have. It makes us addicted to outside affirmation and recognition. If we had the qualities, we would not need this affirmation and confirmation.

> **IDEALIZED IMAGE**
> A personal standard of perfection against which one's actual thinking, behavior, and appearance are compared. An exaggerated and unrealistic view of one's virtues and abilities.

Again, we all have it to some degree, especially if a fixed mindset is in charge. Most of the time, like this woman, we are unaware of it. This is what makes it so dangerous. It's hidden and highly toxic. It's part of the Automatic System's unconscious phenomenon. This is why most people can see through everyone else's idealized image and call them blowhards or narcissists. But a person with the idealized image is not aware of their arrogance. It's like the woman who really believes she is the most beautiful woman in the congregation.

Creating an idealized image is the way we self-love after a crushing defeat due to a bad experience. Unable to build self-confidence on the inside, all our worth lies on the outside. This is why looking good to other people becomes such a stronghold. When our inner value is nonexistent, we become driven to succeed and depend on people to build us up with their confidence in us, which inflates our feelings of significance and power. This leads to measuring ourselves and comparing ourselves with others, which, as Rohr says, becomes the launching pad to inflate the ego using our body image, our job, our education, our clothes, our money, our car, our sexual identity, or our success.[218]

But the inflated ego can be deflated by the smallest insult, which causes us to fight tooth and nail when someone looks down on us or tries to humiliate us. This is how we know the underbelly of the idealized image is shame. It tells us we are not worthy, all the while it demands we get out there and work for affirmation and worthiness. And this game never builds significance, so we use attachments to bolster self-confidence. And the problem is that the solution remains outside of us.

For change to happen, it has to start on the inside. We must decide to make the right choice, even when it is the hardest choice, and this is where most people crumble and fall to pieces. We lack the inward strength to challenge our idealized image because it means we will have to feel deflated before we can heal. Our significance must shift away from our body image, our job, our education, our clothes, our money, our car, our sexual identity, our success, and so on. But unless we empty-out these things that inflate our ego or are our gods, then we can't make room for the true God, the source of love.

To get the life we've always wanted, we must let go of the idealized image. Let go of what people think of you, whether it's real or imaginary. Our identity is not in our success, our body image, our intelligence, our education, etc. We have to die to all these things and stop grasping for and clinging to them—which means we can no longer remain addicted to the praise and approval of others.

Jean Vanier once told a story about God's hands. He described the hands that gently encircle a wounded bird as being hands that are also open to allow movement and freedom to fly. He believes that each of us needs to have both these hands around us. One hand says, "I've got you and I hold you safe because I love you and I'll never be apart from you. Don't be afraid." The other hand says, "Go, my child, find your way, make mistakes, learn, suffer, grow, and become who you need to be. Don't be afraid. You are free and I am always near." Jean Vanier says these two hands are the hands of Unconditional Love.[219] May you experience those two hands today as you create the life you've always wanted and let go of the old, false self.

REFLECTIONS

1. Are you addicted to outside affirmation?

2. To get a new life, we must let go of the old one. What is the scariest part of letting go of the life you have now?

3. Can you describe the two hands of God that surround you?

ALONG THE BARBED WIRE

I read a book by Etty Hillesum, a Jewish prisoner in a Nazi concentration camp. She wrote a whole bunch of letters that chronicled her experience. She writes very candidly about her relationship with God and her growth in the midst of pain. She wrote in one letter, "The misery here is quite terrible and yet, late at night when the day has slunk away into the depths behind me, I often walk with a spring in my step along the barbed wire and then time and again it soars straight from my heart—I can't help it, that's just the way it is, like some elementary force—the feeling that life is glorious and magnificent, and that one day we shall be building a whole new world."[220]

That is one of the most powerful statements. The visual is just unbelievable to me. Even in this confinement, this hell, with barbed wire all around, it hasn't robbed her of joy, of future freedom. She believed the world would one day turn back to love and goodness. And that response can only come from a healthy paradigm.

So, when I read Etty's letter, about feeling glorious and magnificent feelings about life while in a Nazi concentration camp surrounded by barbed wire, I knew it came from a spiritual place. And that was the place God was trying to help me find. Because if we find it, if we can find joy in the midst of suffering, then we've found a new paradigm to see the world from.

Everything in the Bible is pointing us toward our suffering with Christ. "Now if we are children, then we are heirs—heirs of God and co-heirs with Christ, if indeed we share in his sufferings in order that we may also share in his glory" (Romans 8:17). Etty understood this passage. This was where her joy was coming from. We should rejoice in our afflictions. "And we boast in the hope of the glory of God. Not only so, but we also glory in our sufferings, because we know that suffering produces perseverance; perseverance, character; and character, hope. And hope does not put us to shame" (Romans 5:2-4). If we can endure suffering, it leads to character, proven character, and that leads to hope that will not disappoint.

I'm getting it now. Before this moment, I've been trying to tear the barbed wire down in my mind. I wanted something that would catapult me out of my suffering. I wanted something or someone to rescue me from my plight. I wanted to change my circumstances, but I wasn't wanting to change my character. And likewise, if you war against the barbed wire—it will always win. It will lead you to despair. But if while surrounded by barbed wire you can still walk with a spring in your step—you're no longer a victim to it. Your life can still be glorious and magnificent.

Emptying out the old paradigms, the old narratives, the old attachments so that something new can be born is how we step into the future. The key is growth. As Red said in the movie, *Shawshank Redemption,* "Get busy living or get busy dying." If you remember that movie, you know that Red had been contemplating whether or not he wanted to live. There is a huge, paradigm shift between really being alive and just existing. Existence is not living. It's not really being alive. You're just breathing. You're just here. God created us for growth. Hope and growth exist simultaneously. They're enmeshed. So choose to live, even in the midst of pain. Take the step toward a new beginning that will rewrite the ending of your life. Now is the time! Stop believing the lie of the remembering self. Ask yourself, "What emotion is telling the story?" If it is shame and guilt, then stop listening.

Frederick Buechner writes, "Listen to your life. See it for the fathomless mystery that it is. In the boredom and pain of it no less than in the excitement and gladness: touch, taste, smell your way to the holy and hidden heart of it because in the last analysis all moments are key moments and life itself is grace."[221]

REFLECTIONS

1. What emotion is telling your story?

2. Tell of a time in your life when you warred against the barbed wire.

3. What are ways you can reframe what your life looks like right now? For instance, your life could be surrounded by barbed wire and yet you can feel the sunshine on your face, feel the breeze brush through your hair, and see the marvelous colors of the sky.

KENOSIS

Man was added to Him, God not lost to Him; He emptied Himself not by losing what He was, but by taking to Him what He was not.

—AUGUSTINE

Richard Rohr said about St. Francis, "Francis of Assisi was a master of making room for the new and letting go of that which was tired or empty . . . he was ready for absolute 'newness' from God and therefore could also trust fresh and new attitudes in himself."[222] And the same goes for us. Until we let go of the old patterns, we will never experience new freedom. This is at the heart of kenosis—emptying out old patterns. And, I agree, kenosis is mysterious. Kenosis has been more prominent in the Eastern church than the Western. Kenosis is an ancient Greek term primarily found in Christian writings where Paul talked about Christ emptying himself out unto death of the cross." (Philippians 2:7 ASV)

KENOSIS
Emptying oneself out; transcending or detaching of oneself from the world or it's passions

"Have this mind in you, which was also in Christ Jesus: who, existing in the form of God, counted not the being on an equality with God a thing to be grasped, but emptied himself, taking the form of a servant, being made in the likeness of men; and being found in fashion as a man, he humbled himself, becoming obedient even unto death, yea, the death of the cross" (Philippians 2:5-8 ASV).

Kenosis is the concept of emptying ourselves to become full of Christ. The emptying out—the kenosis—is the narrow road so few people choose, because like Adam and Eve, we want to be in control. We want to be our own god which leads us to the patterns of this world. We must empty ourselves and die to ourselves and deny ourselves—however you want to articulate it. This is how we participate with the Divine. But the resistance is so powerful. The ego, which is so needed when we're young to develop our identity and sense of self, must be emptied. But we cling to it like a childhood security blanket. We just don't want to give up our securities, even when they are false and lead us to bondage. And those, I believe, are attachments that end up controlling our lives. It's like a form of idolatry.

Paul said, "I have been crucified with Christ and I no longer live, but Christ lives in me. The life I now live in the body, I live by faith in the Son of God, who loved me and gave himself for me" (Galatians 2:20 NIV). Paul had submitted to kenosis. We must make room for Christ to fill us entirely.

OLD PATTERNS LEAD TO THE SAME OLD BONDAGE

If we believe we are free, when in fact we are not, then our belief is false. Our beliefs are always faulty when our old narratives have formed them, because we look for evidence to support our faulty beliefs. This is why Gideon in Judges 6:38-40 didn't believe God could use him to rescue Israel. He couldn't set himself free from the fear-based paradigm in his head—that if he tried, he would die. "But the Lord said to him, 'Peace! Do not be afraid. You are not going to die.'" Gideon believed he was the weakest member of the weakest clan and feared for his life. This a classic fear-based paradigm that blinded him to other possibilities—he kept looking for evidence to support this paradigm. This is why he asked God for a sign twice. The miracle after putting out the first fleece still left him in doubt, so Gideon questioned the miracle and asked for a new sign—a fleece miracle in a different form.

God was trying to transform Gideon's paradigm, but Gideon just wanted the same old patterns. He was afraid to make a mistake. He could not trust God, even after an angel appeared to him and called him a mighty warrior.

In the same way, the fixed mindset tries to protect you and says— make no mistakes because mistakes can get you killed. A fixed mindset keeps us from participating with the Divine. I know many people who's spiritual lives are about keeping rules and not breaking rules. This may make you a good religious person or Pharisee, but it doesn't lead to participation with the Divine.

Kenosis requires insight into our old narratives. God taught Gideon how to have new insights—which is the discovery of new patterns—by winnowing down his troops before battle. The Lord told Gideon to let any of the warriors go that were timid or afraid—and 22,000 men left leaving 10,000 men. He was teaching Gideon what to look for in an army. The fearful never make valiant warriors, so send them home (Judges 7:3).

Then God tells Gideon to observe the soldiers drinking water. Of the ten thousand, nine thousand seven hundred kneel, bending over the water to drink. But there are three hundred that remain on their feet and bend over the water and catch it in their hands and lap it up.

G. Campbell Morgan writes, "Nine thousand, seven hundred men taking unnecessary time with necessary things. It was a severe ordeal."[223] God told Gideon to send these men home—leaving him only the three hundred men that drank without kneeling. If G. Campbell Morgan is right, then there is another insight—noticing things that are not obvious to others.

Take this example from Gary Klein's book, *Seeing What Others Don't*. Two policemen were stuck in traffic, but they didn't feel impatient. They were on a routine patrol and not much was going on that morning. The older policeman was driving. As they waited for a light to change, the younger policeman glanced at the fancy new BMW in front of them. The driver took a long drag on his cigarette, took it out of his mouth, and flicked the ashes onto the upholstery. The younger policeman couldn't believe that someone would just dump cigarette ashes inside their new BMW. Not the owner of the car. Not a friend who borrowed the car. Possibly a guy who had just stolen the car might do this, so they stopped the BMW and found that it had indeed been stolen. Klein called this an insight,[224] Noticing things that are not obvious to others.

Why would God teach Gideon how to watch for new patterns? New patterns lead to intuition—using already learned patterns to gain insight and discover new patterns.[225] This is important in kenosis because new patterns must be learned then turned into intuition—the use of these learned patterns.

Kenosis is emptying old patterns to see new insights. It's how we renew our minds by no longer transforming to the patterns of this world (Romans 12:2). The patterns of the world must go to make room for new patterns—for new insight—that will lead to intuition, which leads to participation with the Divine (theosis).

Patterns guide our narratives. So, let's reach far back into your old narrative to begin the restoration, because a few walls need to be torn down. Let's start our kenosis here.

REVISIONING THE OLD NARRATIVE

Gideon son of Joash was threshing wheat at the bottom of a winepress to hide the grain from the Midianites. The angel of the Lord appeared to him and said, "Mighty hero, the Lord is with you!" (Judges 6:12). Gideon's old narrative started with weakness and bondage. He was hiding from the Midianites when the angel of the Lord called him a "mighty warrior"—he disagreed passionately. He called himself weak. Next the Lord told him to tear down his father's altar to Baal, build an altar to the Lord and make a burnt offering sacrifice. We know little about Gideon before this moment, but here is what we do know. He was afraid of what his family and the townspeople would think of him if they saw him tearing down the altar to Baal.

Gideon continued to follow old patterns of fear, even though given new instruction from the Lord. Think of the birds in Day 2. Freed from their bondage but still living their old patterns of walking in a circle. Gideon allowed the old pattern of fear to dictate the future. He tore down the altar at night.

Another way to say this is what Os Guinness writes, ". . . old assumptions neutralize the new ones and act as a Trojan Horse in the mind. Finally the point is reached where our minds are not renewed so much as patched up. Or worse, the old presuppositions completely usurp the place of the new."[226]

It was a start for Gideon, but danger still lurked in his mind. He followed God's leading without the act of kenosis. Obedience to God doesn't necessarily mean kenosis has occurred. We can remain attached to old patterns even as a Christian. This is why our paradigms are so important. They can keep us bound, even while Christ declares us free. The consequences Gideon feared about tearing down Baal's altar did not happen. Fear would have to be emptied out for Gideon, for him to achieve personal and military victory.

Gideon underestimated his father's response. He assumed his father would be furious with him and join the townspeople to kill him. But, surprisingly, his father stood up to the townspeople. He told them to let Baal deal with Gideon. His father's response had to be a shock to Gideon. He had errored in forecasting the future. Fear said, "Do it at night. If they find out you did it, they will kill you." But God said, "Do not fear. You will not die."

. We don't go deeper with God and form new patterns because our security is in our old patterns that are attached to false beliefs. We are afraid that without them, our whole life might collapse.

OUR CORE BELIEFS

So, the first step of kenosis is establishing a core belief about God. Klein calls core beliefs "anchors" because they are fairly stable and anchor the way we interpret the other details of our narratives.[227] I think this is a great way to think of God's promises—as the anchors. They anchor us while we establish new patterns to live by.

Os Guinness writes, "But if our picture of God is wrong, then our whole presupposition of what it is possible for God to be or do is correspondingly altered. When the presuppositions are wrong, the picture is wrong."[228] This is why it's so important to begin with the anchor of God's loving presence. Gideon started by asking God why the Lord handed Israel over to the Midianites for seven years—why had they been abandoned? "'Pardon me, my lord,' Gideon replied, 'but if the Lord is with us, why has all this happened to us? Where are all his wonders that our ancestors told us about when they said, 'Did not the Lord bring us up out of Egypt?' But now the Lord has abandoned us and given us into the hand of Midian'" (Judges 6:13). God showed him a new narrative by saving Gideon from his family and the townspeople when he tore down the altar to Baal. It was Gideon's first moment of new insight into God's loving presence, that replaced his idea of God's abandonment.

This was a huge first revelation. It anchored Gideon with a new belief—**God is with me, not against me.** I think kenosis should always start here. It anchors us to God, the lover of our soul. So, the new pattern, the new insight is—I'm worthy of God's best. This has to become the anchor, the core belief or we lose our way through the dark night of the soul. Shame and fear will disintegrate any effort of change without a core belief. Hope is belief and expectation. A faulty core belief is what keeps us tethered to the old pattern, the way the birds were bound by the belief they couldn't be free. So, if the narrative I tell myself is faulty—like Gideon's belief that he was weak and abandoned by God—I remain weak and stuck.

Our core belief about God is the one that carries all the strength. That core belief is what I'm telling myself about God. That's the affirmation that carries all the power. If I don't believe God is for me and wants my best—then shame and fear takeover—because I've made it about our own human strength. Think of Peter sinking after attempting to walk on water in the Gospels[229]. He had his eyes on the winds and the waves and off of his Lord. God's affirmation about us is the most important affirmation of all. But, like Gideon, when bad things happen to good people, we doubt God's goodness. We wonder why God hasn't intervened. If we are not careful, this faulty belief about God's abandonment will cause doubt and fear in us as well.

We must be clear about our idea of a loving God so we don't jump to conclusions when our circumstances seem dire.

We are like the man training to be a paratrooper who was reluctant to jump. He had two chutes and was told, "When you jump, count to ten and then pull the ripcord. If the chute doesn't open, then reach over to the safety chute's ripcord and pull it. Upon landing, a jeep will be there to pick you up and take you back to the base." Once in the air, they had to push the poor reluctant paratrooper out of the plane. As he was going out the door—he didn't count to one, he didn't count to two—he just pulled the ripcord. Nothing happened. As he tumbled through the air, he reached over and pulled the safety chute's ripcord and nothing happened. As he tumbled past some of his fellow paratroopers, they heard him exclaim, "Yeah, and I bet the jeep isn't down there either."

Silly story, but I guess you could say he was jumping to conclusions and his lens of hopelessness had been formed long before he made the jump. His mind jumped to the old pattern. The bad circumstances led to a bad thought, creating doubt about the future. When the negative pattern seemed to fit the circumstances, he doubted good could happen. We usually form our beliefs first, then look for evidence to support our beliefs. This is why we can't trust the mind to help us empty out old patterns at the beginning of kenosis. Our minds will always look for patterns and in the beginning the old patterns are what our minds are looking for. These old patterns are rooted in doubt, fear, and shame.

The beginning of kenosis starts by no longer conforming to the patterns of the world. Then we work on replacing these old patterns by renewing our minds. Why did God start with Gideon smashing the altar of Baal? What old pattern was hindering Gideon in the beginning? Gideon thought that God was not with him—the old pattern of abandonment. David Jackman writes, ". . . just like us, Gideon is busy limiting God's future by his own past."[230]

God is bigger than our small ideas of Him and more gracious to us than our negative perceptions of who He is.[231] Forming the right idea of God is the first step in kenosis.

REFLECTIONS

1. How do you limit your future by the negative patterns of your past?

MANAGING OUR EXPECTATIONS

*I'm not in this world to live up to your expectations
and you're not in this world to live up to mine.*

—BRUCE LEE

A man bought gasoline from the same service station on the same day and at the same time every week. This was back in the day before there were computerized pumps that accepted debit cards, which meant he was forced to interact with the cashier—usually the same cashier. The first time he met the cashier, he absentmindedly asked, "How's it going?"

Without looking up, the attendant responded, "Lousy." It was clear he didn't want to talk about it, so the customer just smiled and gave him his money. The next week, the man asked the same question and the cashier again said, "Lousy." This went on for months. It became a despairing little liturgy they would repeat every week.

Then one day the man asked him again, "How's it going?" and braced for the usual response. But this time the cashier smiled and exclaimed, "Great!" startling the customer.

Astonished, the customer asked, "So, things are improving?"

"Nah," the cashier responded. "I'm just lowering my expectations."

We're not so sure the future holds good things for us. We're not sure how to manage our expectations. We don't want to set them too high. We cling to a brutal realism that steals our joy. We live in the fear of things, lowering our expectations of the future. Or some of us just start expecting the worst. Brené Brown has a term for it—*foreboding joy*—the state of actually being happy but also terrified that something bad is going to happen next. She writes, "Once we make the connection between vulnerability and joy, the answer is pretty straightforward: We're trying to beat vulnerability to the punch. We don't want to be blindsided by hurt. We don't want to be caught off-guard, so we literally practice being devastated or never move from self-elected disappointment."[232]

FOREBODING JOY
The state of actually being happy but also terrified that something bad is going to happen next.

Our low expectations will never allow us to fully feel joyful, which in turn keeps us from God's promises. It's another form of hopelessness. Foreboding joy clips our wings and keeps us from soaring above our problems. The trap we fall into is what psychologists call—*disqualifying the positive*—drawing conclusions only from the negative.

DISQUALIFYING THE POSITIVE
Extreme form of all-or-nothing thinking in which we filter out all the positive evidence about our performance and only attend to the negative.

The opposite of this is what Elie Wiesel, a holocaust survivor, once said, "If you seek a spark, you will find it in the ashes."[233] Everyone has positive things of worth in their ashes. Our jobs may be unrewarding, but our children may bring much joy. To focus only on the negatives of a job is to disqualify the joy of having children. Our financial circumstances may be challenging but our marriage may be great. To focus only on finances, disqualifies a great relationship. The moment we allow the negatives to ruin the positives, life gets out of balance. Relationships end in turmoil. Workouts become drudgery. But there is always hope. God is the master of making something good from something bad—giving us beauty for ashes[234].

The apostle Paul said, "I delight in weaknesses, in insults, in hardships, in persecutions, in difficulties. For when I am weak, then I am strong." Paul delights in weakness because it opens him up to heaven's blessings and strength. But delighting in our weaknesses can be difficult. Albert Camus once said:

> In the midst of hate, I found there was, within me, an invincible love.

> In the midst of tears, I found there was, within me, an invincible smile.

> In the midst of chaos, I found there was, within me, an invincible calm.

> I realized, through it all, that . . . In the midst of winter, I found there was, within me, an invincible summer. And that makes me happy. For it says that no matter how hard the world pushes against me, within me, there's something stronger—something better, pushing right back."[235]

This is the spirit within, the invincible that's stronger than the physical. Always keep your spirit willing. This is resilience, this is grit. Our spirit has the power to see the positive in overwhelming suffering.

RISE UP

The death of our expectations can be a new beginning. Brené Brown writes, ". . . if we care enough and dare enough, we will experience disappointment. But in those moments when disappointment is washing over us and we're desperately trying to get our heads and hearts around what is or is not going to be, the death of our expectations can be painful beyond measure."[236]

In the midst of the death of your expectations, take on God's expectations. "Thy will be done." Keep taking your weakness to God on a daily basis with the expectation that when knocked down, He will help you rise up and continuously rise up. Think of the Itsy-Bitsy spider nursery rhyme. The lyrics go like this:

> The itsy-bitsy spider climbed up the waterspout,
> Down came the rain and washed the spider out,
> Out came the sun and dried up all the rain,
> And the itsy-bitsy spider climbedt up the spout again."[237]

Arthur Freeman writes about this children's song, "Every time the sun comes out, another opportunity exists for the spider to try again. All that has to happen is for the rain to hold off . . . long enough . . . just once . . . and that bug is going to get where it wants to go. That's the real point of this song."[238]

Rise up and keep rising up. This is the only expectation God ever places on us. "Good people might fall again and again, but they always get up" (Proverbs 24:16 ERV). No matter how many times we get knocked down, we rise up. But rising up is never a matter of lowering our expectations but rather replacing them with God's will.

If we feel like we are living under a curse, we will make excuses about why we can't rise up. We may say, "I can't do this. I don't have the strength." But the spirit says, "God's strength is available."

It's like the story of a father and son who were walking and came across a sizable stone along the way. The boy asked his father, "Dad, do you think I'm strong enough to move this stone." The father thought it over for a moment and responded, "Yes, son, you're strong enough, as long as you use every resource that you have." So, the boy tried to move the stone. His first attempt was to pick it up, but it was too big and there was no way he could do that. Then, he tried to push the stone over on its side, but the stone simply wouldn't budge. After a couple of attempts, the boy gave up and said, "Well Dad, I guess you were wrong. I'm not strong enough to move that stone."

But the father said, "Son, you are strong enough—I said you would have to use every resource you had available. You haven't used every resource. You haven't asked me to help you." With that, the son—this time with the assistance of his father—easily pushed the stone over on its side. We must see the stones in life through God's power and vision. "I can do all this through him who gives me strength" (Philippians 4:13). "Help!" might be the greatest prayer we can pray.

Brené Brown says, "I want to be brave with my life. And when we make the choice to dare greatly, we sign up to get our asses kicked. We can choose courage or we can choose comfort, but we can't have both. Not at the same time. Vulnerability is not winning or losing; it's having the courage to show up and be seen when we have no control over the outcome. Vulnerability is not weakness; it's our greatest measure of courage."[239]

REFLECTIONS

1. What expectations do you have for the future? Are you living in joy or fear of the future?

2. Do you ever disqualify the positive?

3. Are you trying to move a large "stone" by yourself in your own strength?

SHAPING OUR LIVES
FOR THE DIVINE

FREEDOM TO LET GO

None are more hopelessly enslaved
than those who falsely believe they are free.

—JOHANN WOLFGANG VON GOETHE

F.W. Boreham writes,

"Professor Herkless, in his Life of Francis d'Assisi, tells us how Francis was torn between the monastic life on the one hand and the domestic life on the other. He longed to be a monk and to dedicate himself to poverty and pilgrimage. And yet he loved a sweet and noble and gracious woman. He wrestled with his alternatives, and at length, through an agony of tears, he chose the cloak and the cowl. But still the lovely face haunted him by cloister and by shrine. And one radiant moonlit night, when the earth was wrapped in snow, the brethren of the monastery saw him rise at dead of night. He went out into the grounds and, in the silvery moonlight, fashioned out of the snow with deft artistic fingers the images of a lovely woman and a group of fair little children. He arranged them in a circle, and sat with them, and, giving rein to his fancy, tasted for one delicious hour the ecstasies of hearth and home, the joys of life and love. Then, solemnly rising, he kissed them all a tearful and final farewell, renounced such raptures for ever, and re-entered the monastery."[240]

He had to come to terms *inwardly* with his *outward* decision to be a friar. I'll explain.

During one of our small groups at Restore, we were discussing Alcoholics Anonymous' "Big Book"[241] and the *quality of our sobriety*. It states that even though we may not be acting out our compulsion or addiction, we can still struggle with some core issues such as regret, resentment, anxiety, or shame—if our inner life hasn't really changed. We remain in a daily struggle with our compulsions and addictions the way St. Francis struggled holding on to his past love.

Outwardly, we appear free, but inwardly we are inflamed with passion. If we continue to battle these negative emotions, relapse is just around the corner. We will reach for food, pornography, alcohol, or any other vice to quench this inward battle.

Let me ask you, "What is the quality of your sobriety—are you free both outwardly and inwardly? Are you filled with regret, remorse, fear, and shame? Or is God transforming those thoughts in your mind, creating serenity?" Remember, that it's an ongoing process that we will be working on with God, for the rest of our lives, because these thoughts and negative beliefs are deeply ingrained. But freedom is possible!

EXTRINSIC MOTIVATION
Award-driven, avoiding punishment, *must* change

INTRINSIC MOTIVATION
Desire to be with God, solution-driven, *want* change

Our motivation to change determines if we can find freedom or not. There are two types of motivation—*extrinsic* motivation and *intrinsic* motivation. Extrinsic motivation is a motivation that is driven by external rewards—which can be positive or negative. If my desire to change is due to negative consequences, then I'm only trying to avoid what I perceive as punishment. If punishment-avoidance is driving our sobriety, it won't be able to sustain itself. We will go back to our prior behavior when the threat is over. However, if my sobriety stems from intrinsic motivation, driven by an internal longing to be with God—then I will want to change, I won't see it as I must change. When God stirs up within me a vision of what I can become, then I'll make the changes necessary to be that person. No longer am I focusing on the problem, but I can now focus on the solution.

Like St. Francis, we must die to the vision causing our pain. This is why he built a family out of snow. He was still hanging on to that vision and it was causing him great pain. But he knew God had a calling on his life. To fully accept it, he had to die once and for all to the vision of what could have been if he'd chosen the domestic life. I see this in people all the time. They struggle with a vision of life God never intended for them. To leave it behind, they must let go and move toward a new God-given vision.

LETTING GO

The key is learning to let go. Henri Nouwen spent some time with The Flying Rodleighs, a trapeze troupe, and described a beautiful picture of letting go. He was fascinated by the way the aerialists moved through the air—flying and catching like elegant dancers. He writes:

> "One day I was sitting with Rodleigh, the leader of the troupe, in his caravan, talking about flying. He said, 'As a flyer, I must have complete trust in my catcher. The public might think that I am a great star of the trapeze, but the real star is Joe, my catcher. He has to be there for me with split second precision and grab me out of the air as I come to him in a long jump.'
>
> 'How does it work?' I asked.

'The secret,' Rodleigh said, 'is that the flyer does nothing and the catcher does everything. When I fly to Joe, I have simply to stretch out my arms and hands and wait for him to catch me and pull me safely over the apron behind the catch bar.'

'You do nothing!' I said, surprised.

'Nothing,' Rodleigh repeated. 'The worst thing the flyer can do is to try to catch the catcher. I am not supposed to catch Joe. It's Joe's task to catch me. A flyer must fly, and a catcher must catch, and the flyer must trust, with outstretched arms that his catcher will be there for him.'

When Rodleigh said this with so much conviction, the words of Jesus flashed through my mind, 'Father, into your hands I commend my Spirit.' Dying is trusting in the catcher. To care for the dying is to say: 'Don't be afraid. Remember that you are a beloved child of God . . . Just stretch out your arms and hands and trust, trust, trust.'"[242]

Part of the reason we revert to old behavior when facing adversity is not trusting God. Faith trusts that He is working behind the scenes and He will catch us if we fall. We must trust that God will fill the void of our lives once the idealized image is gone. Cynthia Bourgeault describes how this happens:

"When we enter [into contemplative prayer], it is like a 'mini-death,' at least from the perspective of the ego . . . We let go of our self-talk, our interior dialogue, our fears, wants, needs, preferences, daydreams, and fantasies . . . We simply entrust ourselves to a deeper aliveness, gently pulling the plug on that tendency of the mind to want to check in with itself all the time. In this sense, meditation is a mini-rehearsal for the hour of our own death, in which the same thing will happen. There comes a moment when the ego is no longer able to hold us together, and our identity is cast to the mercy of Being itself. This is the existential experience of 'losing one's life.'"[243]

We lose our lives for His sake (Luke 17:33). Losing our lives means we let go of the idealized image of ourselves and cast ourselves out into the wide-open space of possibility where God catches us. We silence the ego that is always wanting to control the future by trying to predict it. Our letting go becomes the self-emptying act. We die to our need for the world's affirmation and turn to God's love.

REFLECTIONS

1. What is the "quality of your sobriety"—are you free both outwardly and inwardly?

2. What area in your life do you need to let go of trying to control and turn over to trusting in God?

THE SECRET INGREDIENTS TO HAPPINESS

The happiness of your life depends upon the quality of your thoughts:
therefore, guard accordingly, and take care that you entertain no
notions unsuitable to virtue and reasonable nature.

—MARCUS AURELIUS

We need a sense of higher purpose. Angela Duckworth writes:

> Three bricklayers are asked: "What are you doing?"
>
> The first says, "I am laying bricks."
>
> The second one says, "I am building a church."
>
> And the third says, "I am building the house of God."
>
> The first bricklayer has a job. The second has a career. The third has a calling.[244]

How they viewed their work was the difference. Some of us are in the wrong jobs or the wrong careers, but making a lateral move won't create the life we've always wanted. We need to discover a sense of higher purpose and perhaps finding work that genuinely interests us could be the path forward.

Duckworth conducted a recent survey of 982 zookeepers. This is a profession in which 80% of workers have college degrees and yet only earn an average salary of $25,000 (in 2016). She found that those who identified their work as a calling ("Working with animals feels like my calling in life") also expressed a deep sense of purpose ("The work that I do makes the world a better place"). Zookeepers with a calling were also more willing to sacrifice unpaid overtime hours, to care for sick animals. And the zookeepers with a calling expressed a sense of moral duty ("I have a moral obligation to give my animals the best possible care").[245]

Unlike zookeepers, most of us have felt imprisoned in our jobs. We mope along like the character Frank Wheeler, in the novel *Revolutionary Road*. In the novel, Frank Wheeler works a boring job at Knox Business Machines on the fifteenth floor of the Knox Building. He believes the great advantage of a place like Knox is that you can sort of turn off your mind every morning at nine and leave it off all day and nobody knows the difference. It had taught him new ways of spacing out the hours of the day—"it's almost time to go down for coffee," "it's almost time to go out for lunch," " it's almost time to go home."[246] The danger of Frank Wheeler's life is how he throws away chunks of time each day, enduring life, waiting for the next break instead of living his life to the full.

Most of us live like Frank Wheeler. We find ourselves trapped in uninspiring jobs because we've convinced ourselves that life is merely about paying the bills, and work is something that we have to endure to survive. But the reality is that we have a limited amount of time on earth. The mortality rate is 100%. Most of us never live life to the fullest unless we find out we are going to die. Then we seriously begin to think about doing something which will have lasting impact after we're gone. If we want to find passion and fire oxytocin on an extended release for a greater sense of well-being, then we have to trust God has a higher calling for our lives.

Your calling doesn't have to be a career or job. We can find a higher purpose outside of our workplaces. Stanford developmental psychologist Bill Damon studies purpose in adolescents, and he says, "The purposeful are those who have found something meaningful to dedicate themselves to, who have sustained this interest over a period of time, and who express a clear sense of what they are trying to accomplish in the world and why . . . They know what they want to accomplish and why, and they have taken concerted steps to achieve their ambitions." [247]

Damon believes there are four different types of adolescents. Those with purpose, as I quoted him above, and the rest allocated to the following categories—which I think crosses over to us as adults:

1) **"Disengaged"** (about 25% of young people) – those who have no purpose, apathetic and detached, and show little concern for the world beyond the self.

2) **"The dreamers"** (25%)– who have some aspirations and express ideas about purposes but do little (or nothing) actively to explore any of these ideas.

3) "**The dabblers**" (31%) – those who have engaged in various purposeful activities, but could not find the meaning of these activities beyond the present (and failed to stay committed to any of them for a long time).[248]

Question for you—what category would you fit in? What is your noble purpose?

We all want a higher purpose and meaning, but only a few of us take the risk. We languish with a sense of emptiness. Os Guinness writes, "The trouble is that, as modern people, we have too much to live with and too little to live for. Some feel they have time but not enough money; others feel they have money but not enough time. But for most of us, in the midst of material plenty, we have spiritual poverty."

This is one of the reasons I am writing this book. I see far too many people in spiritual poverty and living a life of emptiness because our fixed mindsets are running the show and telling us nothing can be done. It's too little, too late. But God has given us the brain chemistry to find fulfillment when we cocreate our future with Him. Because life satisfaction comes from chemicals in our brains—dopamine which gives us a sense of temporary pleasure and serotonin which creates a long-lasting feeling of happiness or well-being—fulfillment in life is possible.

Because we fear loss more than we desire gain, we must keep these questions in the forefront of creating our new life: "where am I going?" and "what do I hope to find when I get there?" On the way, "Trust in the LORD with all your heart and lean not on your own understanding; in all your ways submit to him, and he will make your paths straight" (Proverbs 3:5-6 NIV).

We need a purpose that makes us feel like we are making a difference in the world. Let's go back to the bricklayers. They had the same job, but not the same perspective or purpose about their job. The one laying brick did not see it as a purpose for his life, only a paycheck. The second one had a career, but not purpose. Purpose is doing something that interests us and gives us a higher meaning out of life. But, I believe, it also has an element of cocreating something in the world with God. This is where trust enters the formula of extended release of oxytocin to create a greater sense of well-being. We won't always feel that our lives are making a difference, so we must trust. We may even call it having faith. Hebrews 11 is full of saints who, during their time on earth, were unaware of the impact of their actions in the world..Yet they trusted God and took steps of faith even though they were in the dark, so to speak. Faith is an action step.

CREATIVITY AS A SPIRITUAL AWAKENING

A spiritual awakening is necessary for all of us on the journey to deep transformation. It's an important new level of awareness, of consciousness, of a connection to the Divine, to a purpose, a meaning for life, that transcends the daily grind of making money and providing for our families. This connection to the Divine is also a connection to creativity. It's a higher intention. Here's an example. I received an email from a woman, whom I'll call Karen, who is struggling with grief. She's had a horrible tragedy in her life—the death of an adult child. Her life has consisted of getting up and leaving for work at seven each morning and then getting home around six each night—11 hour work days. She's exhausted. She does this day after day after day. Her job is providing income, but it's empty. She says, "I'm living to work, but I'm not living." So, boiled down, she's saying, "I'm alive to work." That's what it feels like to her. Her work is just work. It's financial provision for her life, but it doesn't give her any spark. It doesn't give her connection to something greater than herself. She's just grinding it out day after day, month after month, year after year. Now a tragedy has occurred and she finds herself left with no meaning in life. Is this all there is to life? She believes in God, but has nothing to look forward to at the end of the day. She's been looking for, what I call, an awakening. She then recalls a passion for painting, a creative pursuit, she possessed at one time. She found a simple thing, but something that she really cares about and it is providing a sense of purpose and meaning and empowerment.

Lieberman and Long talk about this awakening in their book, *Molecule of More*:

> "A business executive working in financial services spent his days brooding over stock options, asset derivatives, foreign exchange rates, and other imaginary beasts. He was wealthy and miserable. His misery drove him to see a mental health specialist, and a few months later he had rediscovered his passion for painting, a hobby he had abandoned decades ago. "I can't wait to get home at the end of the day," he told his doctor. "Last night I painted for four hours, and I didn't even realize the time had gone by."[249]

Like this businessman, Karen has found a creative pursuit to live for and it's bringing out the best in her. She rediscovered passion. She has found her reason to be alive.

In the comedy fantasy movie, *Michael*, John Travolta stars as the Archangel Michael, who is sent to Earth to do various tasks, including mending some wounded hearts. In one scene, he's sitting with a dog looking out over a field on a beautiful farm and he talks to the dog about his mission—about how he was sent to earth to help a man get his heart back. And he says something like, "It's a hard thing trying to give a person his heart back." Michael is spot on—it is hard—but it's everything. It's belief and expectancy working in harmony. We believe God for a dream to live for and consequently the Divine in us is awakened. We get our hearts back. We're connected to our heart and our passion. We're alive!

Without passion, life gets stifled. Our talents lay dormant without oxytocin's powerful surge of happiness in the brain. Our brain's H&N chemicals not firing (and the brain releasing CCK's instead) can go on year after year. "The more pain we experience due to these CCK's, the less able we are to feel hope," Dr. Groopman says.[250] No wonder we drink more, we eat more—whatever it is we reach for—we do more. We're reaching for things to distract us, to numb us from the pain of a life without creativity. On the other hand, "Creativity is an excellent way to mix together dopamine and H&N."[251]

Charles Reynolds Brown puts it like this, "Every life is a plan of God. The wise architect never calls for material which will not be needed. Every board, every brick, every shingle, every pane of glass must contribute something to the strength, the beauty, the utility of the building, or it would not be there."[252] God doesn't waste time, effort, or material on us. He created everything intricately and detailed. He knows the plans He has for us. Our part is to believe and trust that His purpose will be fulfilled. **Cocreating with God our new life on this sacred path is the belief we live from (our core values) and the dream we live for (our reward).** You gotta do what makes you come alive inside. Let's look this next week at how God shapes our brains for integration with the Divine.

REFLECTIONS

1. What makes you come alive inside?

2. Does God have a plan for your life? Write a brief paragraph outlining what His plan for your life looks like. Has it changed as you've been progressing through this book?

DELIBERATE PRACTICE

I have no special talent. I am only passionately curious.
—ALBERT EINSTEIN

A story is told of a piano teacher at a musical arts university that was simply and affectionately known as "Herman."

> "One night at a university concert, a distinguished piano player suddenly became ill in the middle of performing an extremely difficult piece. No sooner had the artist retired from the stage, when Herman rose from his seat in the audience, walked onstage, sat down at the piano and with great mastery completed the performance. After everyone had left, one of the students asked Herman how he was able to perform such a demanding piece so beautifully without any notice and with no rehearsal.
>
> Herman replied, 'In 1939, when I was a budding young concert pianist, I was arrested and placed in a Nazi concentration camp. Putting it mildly, the future looked bleak. But I knew that in order to keep the flicker of hope alive that I might someday play again, I needed to practice every day. I began by fingering a piece from my repertoire on my bare board bed late one night. The next night I added a second piece and soon I was running through my entire

repertoire. I did this every night for five years. It so happens that the piece I played tonight at the concert hall was part of that repertoire. That constant practice is what kept my hope alive. Every day I renewed my hope that I would one day be able to play my music again on a real piano, and tonight was that time.'"[254]

Many times, we wait for the door to open to the life we've always wanted. Waiting to see the door open before we ready ourselves to move through it. But this is just a fixed mindset. **A growth mindset puts in the work even when success isn't even on the horizon.** In Jesus' "Parable of the Talents," a man was given one talent (a very large unit of money). Instead of using the talent, he buries it in the ground to protect it because he thinks his master is a shrewd man and will punish him if he does the wrong thing with it. The man with one talent said, "Lord, I knew you to be a hard man, reaping where you have not sown, and gathering where you have not scattered seed" (Matthew 25:24). He had a false view of the character of his master—God. Who told this man that his overseer was a brutal man? It's not clear, but I would put my money on the inner critic. It always tells us to bury all efforts toward growth or we will face judgment. It's a fear-based unhealthy expectation of God's judgment. When the time came for the man with one talent to show what he had achieved, he had nothing to show for it. He wasn't ready for the reward. Think of a talent as our God-given skills, money, assets, resources, abilities—haven't we buried our talent long enough?

THE SUCCESS IS OUT THERE

We must prepare our minds for success. Success is out there. At the appointed time, we will reap success (Galatians 6:9). Without deliberate repeating, reviewing, or thinking about positive things, our brains will prune these unused positive neural pathways within hours or days. Dr.

Joe Dispenza writes in the forward to Dawson Church's book, *Mind Over Matter*,

> "Each time you learn something new, unique possibilities you were not previously aware of open up before you, and as a result you are changed. This is called knowledge, and knowledge causes you to no longer see things the way *they* are. This is the process of learning, and the more you learn, the more you make new synaptic connections in your brain . . . recent studies show that just an hour of focused concentration on any one subject doubles the number of connections in your brain related to that subject. The same research tells us that if you don't repeat, review, or think about what you've learned, those circuits prune apart within hours or days. Thus, if learning is making new synaptic connections, remembering is maintaining those connections.[255]

This is how Herman was so successful on stage when he finally got a chance to play for an audience. He kept his neural connections of how to play beautiful masterpieces on the piano going while inside the concentration camp.

In quantum physics, it would be called the quantum Zeno effect (QZE). "QZE is the repeated effort that causes learning to take place. When you go over and over something, reading it, thinking about it, writing it down, and then repeating this process, you deepen your knowledge and understanding, direct your attention, and grow nerve cells."[256] What you focus on and how you focus alters your brain resulting in structural changes.

QUANTUM ZENO EFFECT
The mental act of focusing attention holds in place brain circuits associated with what is focused on.

Edward Taub, a psychologist at the University of Alabama at Birmingham recruited six violinists, two cellists, and a guitarist—all of whom were right-handed, to have their brains scanned. Taub was interested in the musician's fingers on the left hand, because to play these instruments you need exceptional control of the fingers that move up and down the neck. He also recruited six non-musicians to serve as controls against whom the musicians would be compared. Taub found that the region of the brain controlling the left hand was significantly larger in the musicians than in the non-musicians—and in particular, that the amount of space in the brain controlling the fingers had taken over a section of the brain that was normally devoted to the palm. By contrast, the researchers found no difference between the musicians and non-musicians in the size of the region of the brain controlling the fingers of the right hand.[257]

Anders Ericsson, in his book, *Peak: Secrets from the New Science of Expertise,* comments on Taub's discovery: "The implication was clear: years of practice on a stringed instrument had caused the area of the brain that controls the fingers of the left hand to gradually expand, resulting in greater ability to control those fingers."[258] We know deliberate practice changes the brain. We need to get out of our comfort zones to make changes in our brain. We do this by trying something or learning something that we haven't done or known before.

MAGICAL THINKING VS. DELIBERATE PRACTICE

Many of us speak of what we'd like to become, but we don't take any steps toward becoming that person. We suffer from magical thinking. We believe something outside of us will come along and magically rescue us with no effort on our part. Meanwhile, we just make excuses about why a new life is not possible.

Deliberate practice is how we create new neurological patterns that move us beyond the old nature and toward the new creation (2 Corinthians 5:17). Practice allows us to create new habits to replace the old ones. At times, it won't be easy and it shouldn't be easy. Think of how we change the body through exercise. "As long as the physical exercise is not so strenuous that it strains the body's homeostatic mechanisms, the exercise will do very little to prompt physical changes in the body. From the body's perspective, there is no reason to change: everything is working as it should."[259] But once we push the body beyond homeostatis, different sets of biochemical reactions produce an entirely different suite of biochemical products than the cell would otherwise produce. The cells are not happy with this altered state of affairs and respond by calling up some different genes from the cell's DNA.[260] Exercise with vigorous effort produces change in the cells.

It's the same within the brain. We must strive to change the homeostatic mechanisms of each neuron. If you don't repeat, review, or think about what you've learned, those circuits prune. But if we continue to think the same old thoughts, then the mind has no reason to change.

Anders Ericsson goes on to say, "The fact that the human brain and body respond to challenges by developing new abilities underlies the effectiveness of purposeful and deliberate practice."[261]

Plasticity of the mind makes it possible to change—we are *not* stuck. But we must put in the effort. We must be mindful of what we are thinking, deliberately taking our thoughts captive and replacing them with God's promises. The territory of the mind then grows and new thoughts and creative pursuits are birthed.

REFLECTIONS

1. What would you like your future to look like?

2. How can you prepare your mind for this future? Is it practicing a musical talent or furthering your education? What can you do now to prepare for your future?

FINDING YOUR NORTH STAR

*Obstacles are those frightful things you see
when you take your eyes off your goal.*

—HENRY FORD

On August 5, 1949, Wagner Dodge used fire to fight fire and saved his life. A team of fifteen smokejumpers parachuted into western Montana to control a forest fire. Less than two hours later, twelve of the smoke jumpers lay dead or dying after being trapped by a blowup—a sudden and unexpected firestorm resulting from a collision of fire and winds.

Dodge, the thirty-three-year-old team leader, was respected and loved by his team members. He had served for nine seasons in the Forest Service. While they were hiking down Mann Gulch, Dodge spotted a bit of smoke down at the bottom of his part of the valley. It was a blow-up fire caused by unexpected high winds carrying sparks and embers expanding the fire. Dodge knew this fire would come roaring up the north slope of the valley where he was located with his team, cutting off their escape route and would likely kill them.

Dodge ordered his team to run for safety back to the top of the hill. Dodge and his crew ran for their lives, dropping their tools, hoping they weren't trapped. But as he was running, he looked back and realized they weren't going to make it because the fire had picked up speed and was gaining ground on them.

Two of his men made it to a rocky patch, where the fire would have no fuel, and they survived there. But Dodge couldn't make it there in time, so he had to think of another way to escape. He did something unheard of and unprecedented—he shifted his focus from the fire behind him to the fuel—heavy dry grass—in front of him. He started an escape fire that raced up the slope ahead of him, removing all the grass that would have been the blow-up fire's fuel. Then he dove into the hot ash—the charred center of the escape fire becoming his sanctuary— and the fire passed over him. "As one of the two survivors put it, upon seeing Dodge light a fire, 'we thought he must have gone nuts.'"[262] Dodge reframed what the fire was about to do and found the way of escape. It's another version of the observer effect.

Likewise, psychologists might say it's changing what we think about what we feel—"cognitive restructuring" or "reframing." It's how we are able to neutralize the remembering self. We overcome the remembering self's lie by changing the peak-end rule. Remember the peak-end rule is the worst moment of the experience and its end, which fuels the story the remembering self tells. So to change the peak-end rule requires us to go deeper into our old narratives to discover the positive we can bring forward. For example, we can replace shame's lie of unworthiness with the truth that we are worthy.

COGNITIVE RESTRUCTURING (REFRAMING)
Replace stress-producing thoughts with more balanced thoughts that do not produce stress.

To stop the burning we must go after the fuel. What's fueling the dark emotion (sadness, emptiness, loss, depression, despair, shame, and fear) is a lie of the remembering self. And to discover this lie, we must first tolerate the dark emotion. Through self awareness, we identify the lies of what the remembering self has falsely led us to believe about our ourselves and we courageously share our stories with empathetic witnesses. We hold onto Christ's hand in the most dire and sometimes most painful places and we don't run. We go deeper within and dive into the hot ashes, as Dodge did, to discover the sanctuary of union with God (theosis). It's like the terrifying, but safe passage through the Red Sea. Though painful and challenging to experience, we must first befriend the dark emotion to understand what lie is fueling it. In befriending our pain, we learn from it and unlock our capacity to be transformed by it. It's all about reframing the peak-end rule of shame and pain into positive energy.

S.T.A.R.

To reframe the lie the remembering self is telling, I've devised a tool that will help you co-construct with God a story of redemption. The tool is S.T.A.R. which is the practice of redirecting our thoughts on a daily basis. The letter *S* stands for: **Stop and see where this thought or choice or action is taking you.** Stop and see the positive as well as the negative. Find and surrender to God's love.

Think back to Etty who found joy despite being in a Nazi concentration camp (Day 28). She reframed the lie that she should just be miserable and felt joy in her spirit and hope for the future. She opened her heart to a greater love of self and God, which was a radical paradigm shift from her circumstances.

Likewise, shame forces us into living a life through a false self which causes us to live in despair: "Oh, this is bad. Good people don't do this. If people find out you did this, you'll be exposed for the horrible person you are or the horrible weaknesses you have." And we will do anything to end these feelings. But when we're pulled towards something beautiful, something that actually increases love and goodness, it reveals our true self—the self that always responds to messages of love. I will then choose to follow something that's more life giving, more fulfilling, more beautiful. I will like who I am more. I love who I am more. These positive messages are then intrinsic motivation. It's the gentle invitation of love and grace and there's no greater motivator—it is Christ's message. Our surrender to love creates a radical paradigm shift. Learning to surrender is the journey home.

Gerald May writes, "And there is a particular dimension of grace that is interactive, in which God and person respond mutually to each other's love."[263] That's consecration—not using God to take me out of my pain but saying yes to God's work in my life. It's all about love pulling us towards something beautiful, something affirming, versus being pushed by fear and shame into something we will regret. Love and grace help us surrender our wills to God. So, surrender to love.

The next letter is *T*, which represents *trajectory*. Where am I going with this thought? This choice? This decision? This feeling? Where's this going to take me? What's the trajectory? What's it going to move me towards? The curse is reversed when we create the right trajectory. **The quickest way to change what you feel is to change what you do.**[264]

The next letter is *A,* which is *altitude*. In the old days, when planes got lost, they used the North Star for navigation. Jimmy Stewart plays a pilot in *The Spirit of St. Louis* which is a movie about Lindbergh's history-making transatlantic flight in the purpose-built Spirit of St. Louis high-wing monoplane. During the flight, the pilot got lost in fog out over the ocean. Fog is very dangerous for pilots because they can't see where they're going. They don't know if they're going up or down or in which direction and the disorientation can cause them to crash.

The pilot guided the plane above the clouds and found the North Star which allowed him to get reoriented. Same with us. We get in the fog of shame and we don't know where we are and we wander off our sacred path. We are unable to see our problems through a clear lens. We don't look for the way out. We give up and give in. We believe the lie. We believe we can't transform.

We need to climb up to the highest altitude with God and deal only with Him. Rise above dark moments and discover a blessing by looking on the bright side. We deal with the remembering self by looking through a larger lens with a different perspective. We reach higher for mercy and justice and apply them to the peak-end rule, changing the lie into the truth of God. King David reached higher in Psalm 27:1–7:

> "In you, Lord my God, I put my trust.
>
> I trust in you; do not let me be put to shame, nor let my enemies triumph over me.
>
> No one who hopes in you will ever be put to shame, but shame will come on those who are treacherous without cause.
>
> Show me your ways, Lord, teach me your paths.
>
> Guide me in your truth and teach me, for you are God my Savior, and my hope is in you all day long.
>
> Remember, Lord, your great mercy and love, for they are from of old. Do not remember the sins of my youth and my rebellious ways; according to your love remember me, for you, Lord, are good."

David knew how to exchange the remembering self's lie for God's truth. He knew how to deal only with God. He transformed his old rebellious ways by looking at them through the lens of God's love. When we know how God sees our past, then it ends with a sense of His overwhelming love. We find the silver lining in our dark moments. We understand what Paul wrote in Romans 5:8: "But God demonstrates his own love for us in this: While we were still sinners, Christ died for us."

Then the letter *R* is for *reframe* the moment. This is what smokejumper Wagner Dodge did. He reframed fire. He placed fire in a new or unfamiliar context to create a different outcome. We must do this with the remembering self. We need to reframe the peak-end rule by asking, "How do we want to remember our past? Through the lens of shame or through the lens of God's love?" David reframed his rebellious years and the sins of his youth by allowing God to have the final say so. ". . . according to your love remember me." We apply mercy and justice to our old narratives, then the transformation is complete. Let God have the last say so in the matter and this will give you a new, changed peak-end rule.

Stop and see where this thought or choice or action is taking you

Trajectory of your thought

Altitude—rise above dark moments

Reframe or redirect the moment back onto the higher path

When we are working through kenosis, anything less than a blessing leads to negativity. Under negativity, the pain of emptying out becomes overwhelming and we shut down in the fog of shame and get lost. So, let's deal only with God through the tool of *S.T.A.R.* and it will neutralize the remembering self's fuel of shame, creating a place of sanctuary, which is our goal in theosis. Then like Wagner Dodge, we can jump into the hot ash and find safety. Like the Children of Israel, we can pass through the Red Sea.

REFLECTIONS

1. Discuss your current circumstances by using the *S.T.A.R.* method.

Stop

Trajectory

Altitude

Reframe

OUT OF THE SHADOWS AND INTO THE LIGHT

Keep your face always toward the sunshine—
and shadows will fall behind you.

—WALT WHITMAN

I read an article in *Time* magazine once about life in motels where people live, not for a few days, but on a long-term basis. The reporter called them "motel dwellers," because they've turned motels into habitations. The article mentions a man named Jerald Doherty. Jerald lives at a motel with his dog, Hobo, that has been sheared to look like a lion. Inside the room is a microwave, a tabletop refrigerator, a coffee maker, a hot plate, and a ragged sofa with foam spilling out of the cushions onto a filthy shag carpet. There in the shadow of the motel's flickering neon sign, Jerald dwells. Each night, Jerald drinks a 12-pack of beer. "Best pain-killer I know," he says. Jerald tells the reporter, "When I come home from work and I've had a bad day, I watch the *Lion King*, because it makes me cry."[265]

When I read this, I wondered what part of the *Lion King* makes him cry and why? I went in search of the answer. I sat down and watched the movie trying to see it through the motel dweller's eyes. In the beginning of the movie, Mufasa takes Simba, his son, to the edge of Pride Rock and shows him the kingdom. Simba asks about the region of the shadows. He is told not to go there. Eventually, Simba goes into the shadows anyway and finds evil. Mufasa rescues his son. Soon afterwards, Mufasa is killed by his evil brother, Scar. Scar tells Simba it is his fault. He tells him to run and never come back.

Why does Jerald Doherty cry? I believe he cries because he doesn't have a father to come into the shadows to get him out. He cries because he thinks there's no way out of the shadows and for some reason, he believes it is his fault. I wonder why this poor man puts himself through this on bad days? Why watch something that makes him cry? It must be because somewhere deep inside—*hope* still abides. He hasn't given up yet. But he's stuck and doesn't know how to get beyond the lie of the ego that tells him he is all alone and no one is coming to rescue him from the shadows.

Think of the story in the Bible where a man that sat beside the Pool of Bethesda for thirty-eight years because he had no one to help him into the water. He couldn't see a way for it to happen, but he remained at the pool (John 5). Somewhere inside him hope still existed. Don't believe the ego's lie that you are not enough. The fact that you are reading this book means hope is still alive in you. I am here to assist you in finding that hope and becoming unstuck.

The first step out of the shadows is to know condemnation is the ego's number one tool to use against you. It tells us to remain hidden in the shadows. It says, "It's okay if you want to watch a movie about redemption, but don't you dare believe you can experience it." Brené Brown says that the way to take off the ego's mask is by believing that we are enough..[266]It's worthiness versus shame. I believe Jerald Doherty is feeling more shame than worthiness. It's one thing to understand redemption and another thing to allow yourself to experience it. The ego always tells us the cost is too great. "You will be rejected and scorned," ego says. "So, stay hidden."

What if I told you that the ego's death is really a *sacred death*? In this death, hope breaks through your anguish and grief. Hope leads you to the pain, so you can empty it out letting the divine move in and rescue you. Sometimes it takes a breakdown for a breakthrough so God can do for you what you cannot do for yourself.

Richard Rohr writes, "The ego and the false self hate change more than anything else in the world, and the mind is their primary control tower."[267] No wonder Jesus said we had to lose ourselves to find ourselves (Matthew 10:39). We have to let go of the ego. Removing ego from the primary control tower leads to transformation. Once the ego is detected and removed, we can see with a whole new attitude. This is what Paul means by being made new in the attitude of our minds (Ephesians 4:23). We take on a new mind. We take on the mind of Christ. We are *in* Christ. The "I" moves to the middle of "Who I Am." Remember Christ said in John 8:58, ". . . before Abraham was born, I am!"

Renewing our minds is possible. Dr. Caroline Leaf writes, "Our brain is changing moment by moment as we are thinking. By our thinking and choosing, we are redesigning the landscape of our brain."[268] When we choose the right thoughts of love, then we change and become more like Christ. If we are viewing life through an old shame-based paradigm, then the paradigm must change for us to experience freedom.

The ego's sacred death starts with vulnerability. We admit we need God to come into our shadowland and get us out because we've made a mess of things. We admit our weaknesses and ask for His strength in the areas where pain is the greatest. Richard Rohr writes, "We have been graced for a truly sweet surrender, if we can radically accept being radically accepted—for nothing! 'Or grace would not be grace at all'! (Romans 11:6)."[269]

REFLECTIONS

1. Do you run from vulnerability or do you embrace it?

2. Is there an area of weakness, shame, or pain where you need to ask God for His strength?

WOOP IT!

*Between the great things we cannot do and the small things
we will not do, the danger is that we shall do nothing.*

—ADOLPHE MONOD

Stephen Ambrose wrote a best-selling book on the Lewis and Clark expedition titled, *Undaunted Courage*. Captain Meriwether Lewis and Second Lieutenant William Clark led an expedition to cross the newly acquired western portion of the country after the Louisiana Purchase. After two years of battling nearly insurmountable problems—hunger, fatigue, desertion, hostile enemies, severe illness, and death—the party had reached the headwaters of the Missouri River. All their advance information had led them to believe that once they reached the continental divide, they would have about a half-day portage (carrying their boats), then reach the waters of the Columbia River and be able to float safely to the Pacific Ocean. They were on their way to hero status. The hard part was behind them. Or so they thought.

Lewis left the rest of the party behind to climb the bluffs that would enable them to see the other side, hoping to see the waters that would carry them the rest of the way. Imagine what he felt when, rather than seeing a gentle sloping valley as he expected, instead he was the first non-native to lay eyes on the Rocky Mountains!

John Ortberg writes, "What do you do when you think your biggest problems are behind you, only to find out you have just been warming up? Eventually, crossing the Rocky Mountains would be perhaps the supreme achievement of the whole trip. But what a challenge."[273]

If we were faced with this kind of challenge, how would we stay motivated to keep journeying on? Where would we find the motivation?

WILLPOWER IS NOT KING

Anders Ericsson and Robert Pool, in their book, *Peak: Secrets From the New Science of Expertise,* say that it may seem natural to assume that some people possess the rare gift of willpower and the rest of us just lack willpower. But that would be a mistake because *there is little scientific evidence for the existence of a general "willpower" that can be applied in any situation.* The available evidence indicates that willpower is a very situation-specific attribute. People find it much easier to push themselves in some areas than in others. It goes back to relevance. Our brains distribute their resources based on relevance. For example, you may like tennis. I may hate it. Therefore, situation-specific attributes will take you further in tennis. You enjoy it more. This creates motivation. And motivation is quite different from willpower. The obvious question becomes: *What factors shape motivation?* Ericsson and Pool write:

> "There are some interesting parallels between improving performance and losing weight. People who are overweight generally have little difficulty starting a diet program, and they will generally lose some weight on it. But almost all of them will eventually see their progress stop, and most of those will gradually regain the weight they lost, putting them right back where they started. The ones who are successful in losing weight over the long run are those who have successfully redesigned their lives, building new habits that allow them to maintain the behaviors that keep them losing weight in spite of all of the temptations that threaten success."[274]

WILLPOWER
Control exerted to do something or restrain impulses.

MOTIVATION
The reason(s) one has for acting or behaving in a particular way.

This is key to everything we've learned about habits and the brain. If you establish habits that operate automatically, eliminating the need for conscious decision-making, then you will remain motivated. This is why habit change inside the Automatic System transforms our lives.[275]

As long as we are working on behavior modification and not redesigning our lives, we will feel the tug of temptation and, eventually, experience failure.

Remember how Herman, the Holocaust survivor, played the piano that night without having to give it any thought. He had built new neural pathways practicing the music he loved and the quantum Zeno effect kicked in. His brain became what he focused on. The result is structural change in the brain. We can do the same. We need our new automated habits to create new neural pathways.

WISH
Passive feeling or desire for something that is not easily attainable; want something that probably will not happen.

HOPE
Feeling of expectation and desire for a certain thing to happen which leads to action.

Dr. Shane Lopez, author of the book *Making Hope Happen*, says, "Hope is half optimism. The other half is the belief in the power that you can make it so. There is a profound difference between hoping and wishing. Wishing encourages passivity, whereas hope represents an active stance . . . Wishing is the fantasy that everything is going to turn out OK. Hoping is actually showing up for the hard work."[277]

Commit to making a new life with new habits. To do this, let's try what Gabriele Oettingen calls "the WOOP method."

WOOP

Oettingen, in her book *Rethinking Positive Thinking*, writes, "Simply put, by adding a bit of realism to people's positive imaginings of the future, mental contrasting enables them to become dreamers *and* doers."[278]

Oettingen has developed a mental contrasting process she calls "WOOP," which stands for—Wish, Outcome, Obstacle, Plan. She developed WOOP to help people move beyond just having positive thoughts about change to actually transforming. She believes fantasizing about change can actually harm your outcome.

Create a **W**ish
Visualize the **O**utcome
Identify **O**bstacle
Create an if-then **P**lan

She discovered that fantasizing can actually harm the outcome by asking women about shoes. She recruited 164 female college students and divided them into two groups. Then invited the women to fill out questionnaires on a computer and daydream about high heels. For three minutes, a message on the screen asked the women to imagine themselves all dressed up in fabulous high heels. They were then prompted to jot down their spontaneous thoughts and daydreams. One woman wrote, "They make me feel taller, more sophisticated and more confident. The heels make my legs look longer and thinner."

When the three minutes were up, one group was instructed to generate even more positive thoughts about wearing high heels. The other group was asked to generate and write down some negative thoughts about wearing high heels. One woman wrote: "My feet hurt really bad and I trip once or twice while wearing them. I want to take them off just to ease the pain they cause and a blister is forming on my right foot."

Then Oettingen took their systolic blood pressure readings to discover how energized or motivated each participant was by daydreaming. They wanted to see if dreaming about shoes would render these women more or less energized.

At the outset, the two groups didn't differ in their blood pressure. But after their imagery exercise, women who had only positively fantasized about wearing high heels showed lower systolic blood pressure. By contrast, the women whose positive fantasies they'd quelled by asking them to negatively question their heels showed no change in blood pressure. Oettingen writes,

> "It's remarkable that positive fantasies help us relax to such an extent that it shows up in physiological tests. If you want to unwind, you can take some deep breaths, get a massage, or go for a walk—but you can also try simply closing your eyes and fantasizing about some future outcome that you might enjoy. But what about when your objective is to make your wish a reality? The *last* thing you want to be is relaxed. You want to be energized enough to get off the couch and lose those pounds or find that job or study for that test, and you want to be motivated enough to stay engaged even when the inevitable obstacles or challenges arise. We've seen that the principle of "Dream it. Wish it. Do it." does not hold true, and now we know why: in dreaming it, you undercut the energy you need to do it. You put yourself in a temporary state of bliss, calmness—and lethargy."[279]

Positive thoughts won't transform us. They may in fact undercut our energy to blast through the negative to the actual fulfillment of transformation.

Scripture says that Christ endured the cross for the joy that was set before him, scorning its shame (Hebrews 12:2). So, it wasn't just joy that helped Christ fulfill his plan. He had to scorn shame as well, plunging to the depths of disgrace. He held both joy and shame in balance. He knew he had to drink the cup of suffering to fulfill his plan of redemption for the world. It was bittersweet, as all things worth achieving are in life.

Because relying solely on dreams failed to assist individuals in realizing their potential, Oettingen transitioned to a new hypothesis she named "Mental Contrasting." "I reasoned that the best way to get people up and moving was to ask them to dream and then to confront them right away with the realities that stood in the way of their dreams . . . If I could ground fantasies in a reality through mental contrasting, I might be able to circumvent the calming effects of dreaming and mobilize dreams as a tool for prompting directed action."[280]

To implement Mental Contrasting or WOOP, follow these steps. Reflect on your wish or dream, envisioning what you desire to come true and contrast it with the reality of your current situation, examining how it aligns with your dream. Experiencing this contrast underscores the need for action. It vividly illustrates that progress towards your goal requires action.

You will inevitably encounter obstacles along your path. Identify potential obstacles that could get in the way. Develop a plan for addressing each obstacle as it arises.

So, let's end this study where we started—what is possible for you? What kind of life do you really want? To get you further down this road, let's institute what Oettingen seems to be advocating in WOOP—Wish, Outcome, Obstacle, Plan. Take some time and think through where you want life to take you by using her WOOP strategy.

REFLECTIONS

Let's finish our time together by doing Oettingen's WOOP exercise.

1. What is the life you **W**ish for?

2. What is the best **O**utcome?

3. What is your **O**bstacle:

4. What is your *If-then* **P**lan:

ENDNOTES

1 Stephen Covey, *The 7 Habits of Highly Effective People*, (New York: Simon & Schuster, 2004), 39.

2 Dr. Joe Dispenza, *Breaking the Habit of Being Yourself*, (New York: Hay House, 2012), 86.

3 D. Martyn Lloyd-Jones, *Romans: Exposition of Chapter 12 Christian Conduct*, (Carlisle, PA: Banner of Truth Trust, 2015), 100.

4 James Clear, *Atomic Habits*, (New York: Avery, 2018), 33.

5 Dan P. McAdams, "The Psychology of Life Stories." Review of General Psychology, 2001, Vol. 5, No. 2, 100-122. https://www.sesp.northwestern.edu/docs/publications/430816076490a3ddfc3fe1.pdf

6 Dan P. McAdams, 100.

7 Davon Huss, "Unusual Banquet," Sermon Central, Oct 22, 2013. https://www.sermoncentral.com/sermon-illustrations/83543/unusual-banquet-by-davon-huss

8 Covey, 39.

9 Covey, 40.

10 Viktor Frankl, *Man's Search for Meaning*, (Verlag für Jugend und Volk, Austria, 1946).

11 Dr. Joe Dispenza, *You Are the Placebo,* (New York: Hay House, 2014), 51-52.

12 Dispenza, *Breaking the Habit of Being Yourself,* 22.

13 Brené Brown, "Own Our History. Change the Story." Brené Brown, June 18, 2015. https://brenebrown.com/blog/2015/06/18/own-our-history-change-the-story/

14 Carol S. Dweck, *Mindset: The New Psychology of Success*, (New York: Ballantine Books, 2016), 15-16.

15 Richard Rohr, *Falling Upward : A Spirituality for the Two Halves of Life*, (Jossey-Bass, 2011)

16 Dweck, 16.

17 Chuck Swindoll, "Think It Over, " Insight, January 25, 2015. https://www.insight.org/resources/daily-devotional/individual/think-it-over

18 Dispenza, *You Are the Placebo*, 161.

19 Gerald May, *Addiction & Grace*, (San Francisco: HarperSanFrancisco, 1991), 90.

20 Rob Bell, *Velvet Elvis*, (Grand Rapids, MI: Zondervan, 2005), 146.

21 Hengchen Dai, Katherine L. Milkman, Jason Riis, *The Fresh Start Effect: Temporal Landmarks Motivate Aspirational Behavior.* (Management Science. 2014) http://dx.doi.org/10.1287/mnsc.2014.1901

22 Haddon Robinson, *Decision Making by the Book*, (Wheaton, Illinois: Victor Books, 1991), 9.

23 Frankl, *Man's Search for Meaning*

24 Dweck, 159.

25 Dr. Kevin Elko and Rev. Duane Thompson, "Believing is Seeing: Ten Steps to a Mindset That Will Transform Your Direction and Your Life," (Pelham, AL: Whitman Publishing, 2020), 86.

26 Covey, 81.

27 Christopher Shea, "Mindful Exercise," New York Times, December 9, 2007. https://www.nytimes.com/2007/12/09/magazine/09mindfulexercise.html

28 Katy Milkman, *How to Change: The Science of Getting from Where You Are to Where You Want to Be*, (Portfolio, 2021).

29 Dweck, 25.

30 Charles Duhigg, *The Power of Habit*, (New York: Random House, 2012), 273.

31 Rosamund Stone Zander and Benjamin Zander, *The Art of Possibility*, (New York: Penguin Books, 2000), 19.

32 Gary Klein, *Seeing What Others Don't*, (New York: Public Affairs, 2013), 173.

33 Milkman. *How to Change*.

34 Michaela Barnett, "Good Habits, Bad Habits: A Conversation with Wendy Wood," Behavioral Scientist, Oct. 14, 2019. https://behavioralscientist.org/good-habits-bad-habits-a-conversation-with-wendy-wood/

35 Milkman. *How to Change*.

36 Richard Thaler and Cass Sunstein, *Nudge: Improving Decisions About Health, Wealth, and Happiness*, (Yale University Press 2008), 20.

37 Kahneman, 11.

38 Thaler and Sunstein, 20.

39 Thaler and Sunstein, 19-20.

40 Kahneman, 11.

41 Kahneman, 23.

42 Kahneman, 26.

43 Duhigg, 20.

44 Curt Thompson, *The Anatomy of the Soul*, (Carol Stream, IL: Tyndale, 2010), 53.

45 Portia Nelson, *There's a Hole in My Sidewalk: The Romance of Self-Discovery*, (Los Angelese: Beyond Words Publishing, Inc., 1977), 2.

46 Kahneman, 81.

47 Caroline Leaf, *Switch on Your Brain*, (Grand Rapids: Baker Books, 2013), 64.

48 David Eagleman, *Livewired: The Inside Story of the Ever-Changing Brain*, (New York: Pantheon Books, 2020), 147.

49 Eagleman, 118.

50 Wendy Wood, *Good Habits, Bad Habits*, (New York: Farrar, Straus and Giroux, 2019), 18.

51 Roger Martin, *The Opposable Mind*, (Boston: Harvard Business Press, 2009), 50.

52 Lisa K. Libby and Richard P. Eibach, "Looking Back in Time: Self-Concept Change Affects Visual Perspective in Autobiographical Memory." Journal of Personality and Social Psychology 2002, Vol. 82, No. 2, 167-179. https://resolver.scholarsportal.info/resolve/00223514/v82i0002/167_lbitscavpiam.xml

53 Libby and Eibach, 168.

54 Eagleman, 121.

55 Covey, 74

56 David Kindy, "The Accidental Invention of Play-Doh," Smithsonian Magazine, November 12, 2019. https://www.smithsonianmag.com/innovation/accidental-invention-play-doh-180973527/

57 Libby and Eibach, 167-179.

58 Steven Kotler and Jamie Wheal, *Stealing Fire*, (New York: Dey St, 2017), 38.

59   Dispenza, *Breaking the Habit of Being Yourself*, 22.

60   D. Martyn Lloyd-Jones, 100.

61   Adam Grant, *Think Again*, (New York: Viking Books, 2021), 62-63.

62   Clear, 32.

63   Richard Rohr, *Immortal Diamond*, (San Francisco, CA: Jossey-Bass, 2013), 51.

64   Wood, *Good Habits, Bad Habits*, 14.

65   Wood, *Good Habits, Bad Habits*, 26.

66   "New Insights into Americans' Perceptions and misperceptions of Obesity Treatments, and the Struggles Many Face," NORC at the University of Chicago, October 2016, http://www.norc. org/PDFs/ASMBS%20Obesity/Issue%20Brief%20B_ASMBS%20NORC%20Obesity%20 Poll.pdf

67   Duhigg, 36.

68   Duhigg, 51.

69   Wood, *Good Habits, Bad Habits*, 18.

70   "The Science of Changing Habits with Professor Wendy Wood," The Weekend University Podcast, Jan. 7, 2022. https://youtu.be/F8aYfx8Y16w?feature=shared

71   Wood, *Good Habits, Bad Habits*, 107.

72   Duhigg, 20.

73   Wood, *Good Habits, Bad Habits*, 104.

74   Wood, *Good Habits, Bad Habits*, 107.

75   Eagleman, *Livewired*, 151-152.

76   Covey, 79.

77   Eagleman, *Livewired*, 151-152.

78   Eagleman, *Livewired*, 151-152.

79   Scott Barry Kaufman, "How to Make Positive Changes that Stick," The Psychology Podcast, May 20, 2020.

80   Wood, *Good Habits, Bad Habits*, 130.

81   Kahneman, 81.

82   Thaler and Sunstein, 23.

83   Thaler and Sunstein, 185-186.

84   Eagleman, *The Brain*, 142.

85   Clear, 24.

86   Homer, *The Odyssey*. (London, New York: W. Heinemann; G.P. Putnam's sons, 1919)

87   Paul Tillich, *The Shaking of the Foundations*, (New York: Charles Scribner's Sons, 1948), 96.

88   Richard Rohr, *The Naked Now*, (New York: Crossroad Publishing Company, 2019), 23.

89   Rohr, *The Naked Now*, 29-30.

90   Halford E. Luccock, *Unfinished Business*, (Harper & Brothers, 1956) https://bible.org/illustra-tion/flagstaff-flooding

91   Leaf, 105.

92   Rohr, *The Naked Now*, 63.

93   D. Martyn Lloyd-Jones, 133.

94   Paul Harvey, *For What It's Worth*, (New York: Bantam Books, 1991), 31.

95 National Interagency Fire Center. 2016. https://web.archive.org/web/20190627155043/https://www.nifc.gov/policies/policies_documents/StandardsInteragencyHotshotCrewOps.pdf

96 Grant, 6.

97 Grant, 7.

98 NWCG - National Wildfire Coordinating Group, "WFSTAR Part 2, 1994 South Canyon Fire on Storm King Mountain 13:20," Apr 6, 2018. https://www.youtube.com/watch?v=eOP8iH-KeA_8

99 "The Second Gaze," Center for Action and Contemplation, January 7, 2018. https://cac.org/the-second-gaze-2018-01-07/

100 Grant, 5.

101 Eagleman, *The Brain*, 99.

102 Kristen Meinzer, "Surprise! Why the Unexpected Feels Good, and Why It's Good For Us," The Takeawa, April 1, 2015. https://www.wnycstudios.org/podcasts/takeaway/segments/surprise-unexpected-why-it-feels-good-and-why-its-good-us

103 Kristen Meinzer, "Surprise! Why the Unexpected Feels Good, and Why It's Good For Us"

104 Chip Heath and Dan Heath, *Made to Stick: Why Some Ideas Survive and Others Die*, (New York: Random House, 2008), 68.

105 Charles R. Swindoll, *Moses*, (Nashville: Thomas Nelson, 1999), 97-98.

106 Kristen Meinzer, "Surprise! Why the Unexpected Feels Good, and Why It's Good For Us"

107 Heidelberg Herald. "Habits, " Sermon Illustrations, June 14, 1992. http://www.sermonillustrations.com/a-z/h/habits.htm

108 Kaufman, *The Psychology Podcast*, May 20, 2020.

109 "The Science of Changing Habits with Professor Wendy Wood"

110 Wood, W., & Neal, D.T., 71-83.

111 May, 150.

112 Amy Fleming, "The Science of Craving," The Economist 1843 Magazine, May-June 2015. https://www.economist.com/1843/2015/05/07/the-science-of-craving

113 Daniel Z. Lieberman and Michael E. Long, *The Molecule of More: How a Single Chemical in Your Brain Drives Love, Sex, and Creativity—and Will Determine the Fate of the Human Race*, (Dallas, TX: BenBella Books, 2018), 16.

114 Kent C Berridge, Terry E Robinson, and J Wayne Aldridge, "Dissecting components of reward: 'liking', 'wanting', and learning," National Library of Medicine, 2009. https://www.ncbi.nlm.nih.gov/pmc/articles/PMC2756052/

115 Paul J. Zak, "The Neuroscience of Trust," Harvard Business Review: Employee Engagement | The Neuroscience of Trust, January-February 2017. https://hbr.org/2017/01/the-neuroscience-of-trust

116 Lieberman and Long, 35.

117 Christy Kennedy, "Understanding Three Types of Empathy for Emotional Intelligence," LinkedIn, Feb. 16, 2018. https://www.linkedin.com/pulse/understanding-three-types-empathy-emotional-christy-kennedy

118 Paul J. Zak, *Trust Factor: The Science of Creating High-Performance Companies*, (New York: American Management Association, 2017), 17.

119 Paul J. Zak, T*he Moral Molecule: The Source of Love and Prosperity*, (New York: Dutton, 2012), 151.

120 Covey, 113.

121 University of Southern California. "Habit makes bad food too easy to swallow." ScienceDaily, September 1, 2011. www.sciencedaily.com/releases/2011/09/110901135108.htm

122 "The Science of Changing Habits with Professor Wendy Wood,"

123 Kahneman, 53.

124 Dispenza, *Breaking the Habit of Being Yourself*, 22.

125 Thaler and Sunstein, 3-4.

126 Lieberman and Long, 9.

127 Lieberman and Long, 8.

128 Lieberman and Long, 9 and xvii.

129 D. Martyn Lloyd-Jones, 128.

130 W. E. Hill (William Ely), "My wife and my mother-in-law." Library of Congress, November 6, 1915. http://loc.gov/pictures/resource/ds.00175/

131 Eagleman, The Brain, 111.

132 Eagleman, The Brain, 111.

133 C.S. Lewis, Mere Christianity, (New York: Touchstone, 1996), 176.

134 Clear, 34.

135 Thomas Merton, *New Seeds of Contemplation*, (New York: New Directions Book, 2007), 16-17; 21.

136 Covey, 39.

137 Roger N. Shepard. "Turning the Tables," *Mind Sights*, 1990. https://en.wikipedia.org/wiki/Shepard_tables#/media/File:Table_shepard.preview.jpg

138 Thaler and Sunstein, 17.

139 Thaler and Sunstein, 23.

140 Mark 8:18

141 Karl E. Weick and Kathleen M. Sutcliffe, *Managing the Unexpected*, (San Francisco: John Wiley & Sons, 2007), 26.

142 Grant, 42.

143 Tierney and Baumeister, 13.

144 Josh David, "This Is Your Brain's Default Setting–Here's How And When To Change It," Fast Company 8.23.16. https://www.fastcompany.com/3063080/overconfidence-is-your-brains-default-setting-heres-how-to-override-it

145 David.

146 Tierney and Baumeister, 13.

147 Wood, *Good Habits, Bad Habits*, 26.

148 Freeman and DeWolf, 53.

149 Eagleman, Livewired, 194.

150 Eagleman, Livewired, 194.

151 Weick and Sutcliffe, 26.

152 Timothy R. Jennings, M.D., *The God-Shaped Brain*, (Downer's Grove, IL: InterVarsity Press, 2013), 55-56.

153 Jennings, 55.

154 Jennings, 56.

155 Ellicott's Commentary for English Readers, Online Parallel Bible Project, 2007. https://bible-hub.com/commentaries/ellicott/exodus/4.htm

156 Pulpit Commentary, Online Parallel Bible Project, 2007. https://biblehub.com/commentaries/pulpit/exodus/4.htm

157 Clear, 49.

158 Rohr, *The Naked Now*, 50.

159 Covey, 86.

160 Tierney and Baumeister, 26.

161 "Braveheart" 1995. American Rhetoric: Movie Speech. https://www.americanrhetoric.com/MovieSpeeches/specialengagements/moviespeechbraveheart.html

162 Chris Hurn, "Stuffed Giraffe Shows What Customer Service Is All About," Huffpost, May 17, 2012. https://www.huffpost.com/entry/stuffed-giraffe-shows-wha_b_1524038

163 Kahneman, 381.

164 Kahneman, 381.

165 Kahneman, 385.

166 Brené Brown, "Own Our History. Change the Story."

167 Clear, 62.

168 Miriam Greenspan, *Healing Through the Dark Emotions*, (Boston, MA: Shambhala, 2003), 80.

169 A. G. Greenwald, "The totalitarian ego: Fabrication and revision of personal history. American Psychologist," 35(7), 603–618, 1980. http://www.psych.purdue.edu/~willia55/392F-%2706/Greenwald.pdf

170 Greenwald, "The totalitarian ego: Fabrication and revision of personal history. American Psychologist"

171 Lisa K. Libby and Richard P. Eibach, "Looking back in time: self-concept change affects visual perspective in autobiographical memory." J Pers Soc Psychol. 2002 Feb;82(2):167-79. PMID: 11831407, 167.

172 Libby, Eibach, 169.

173 "R. D. Jones And His Sewing Machine," Maineiac. https://maineiac.com/index.php/jokes/on-the-job-jokes/1085-r-d-jones-and-his-sewing-machine

174 John Tierney and Roy F Baumeister, *The Power of Bad: How the Negativity Effect Rules Us and How We Can Rule It*, (New York: Penguin, 2019), 25.

175 Tierney and Baumeister, 22.

176 Tierney and Baumeister, 32.

177 Adam Alter and Hal Hershfield, "People search for meaning when they approach a new decade in chronological age," PNAS, November 17, 2014. https://www.pnas.org/doi/10.1073/pnas.1415086111

178 Daniel H. Pink, *When: The Scientific Secrets of Perfect Timing, (New York: Riverhead Books, 2018), 147.*

179 Covey, 74.

180 Constantine Sedikides, Tim Wildschut,Jamie Arndt, and Clay Routledge, "Nostalgia: past, present, and future," Current Directions in Psychological Science, Vol. 17, No. 5, 2008, 304-307. https://www.researchgate.net/publication/313213209_Nostalgia_past_present_and_future

181 Sedikides, Wildschut, Arndt, and Routledge, 307.

182 John DiPrete, "The Benefits of Nostalgia," Psych Central, Sept 16, 2018. https://psychcen-tral.com/blog/the-benefits-of-nostalgia#1

183 C. Sedikides, T. Wildschut, J. Arndt, and C. Routledge, 308.

184 Tierney and Baumeister, 199.

185 Kahneman, 381.

186 C. Sedikides, T. Wildschut, J. Arndt, and C. Routledge, 307.

187 "Hope: Bits & Pieces," Sermon Illustrations, July 1991. http://www.sermonillustrations.com/a-z/h/hope.htm

188 Tierney and Baumeister, 11.

189 Clear, 15.

190 Duhigg, 112.

191 Teresa M. Amabile and Steven J. Kramer, "The Power of Small Wins." Harvard Business Review, May. 2011. https://hbr.org/2011/05/the-power-of-small-wins

192 Amabile and Kramer, "The Power of Small Wins."

193 Tierney and Baumeister, 25.

194 Eagleman, *Livewired*, 214.

195 Daniel H. Pink, *Drive: The Surprising Truth About What Motivates Us*, (New York: Riverhead Books, 2009), 159.

196 Eugene H. Peterson, *Run with the Horses: The Quest for Life at Its Best*, (IVP, 2022)

197 Chip and Dan Heath, *Switch: How to Change Things When Change is Hard*, (New York: Currency, 2010), 74-75.

198 Dispenza, *You Are the Placebo*, 234.

199 Eugene Peterson, *Run with the Horses*

200 Dispenza, *You Are the Placebo*, 105.

201 Dr. Jerome Groopman, *The Anatomy of Hope*, (New York: Random House, 2005), 179.

202 Groopman, 218.

203 Dispenza, *You Are the Placebo*, 165.

204 Dispenza, *You Are the Placebo*, 200.

205 Groopman, 193.

206 Martin Seligman, *Learned Optimism*, (New York: Pocket Books, 1998), 48-9.

207 May, 14.

208 May, 3.

209 Dispenza, *Breaking the Habit of Being Yourself*, 4.

210 Brené Brown, *Daring Greatly*, (New York: Avery, 2012), 45.

211 Thompson, 23.

212 Curt Thompson, *The Soul of Shame*, (Downers Grove, Illinois: IVP Books, 2015), 94.

213 Richard Rohr, *Immortal Diamond*, (San Francisco, CA: Jossey-Bass, 2013), 28.

214 John Bradshaw, *Healing the Shame That Binds You*, (Deerfield Beach, Florida: Health Communications, Inc., 1988), 30.

215 Thompson, *The Soul of Shame*, 141.

216 A.W. Tozer, *I Talk Back to the Devil*, (Camp Hill, PA: Christian Publications, 1990), 7.

217 Karen Horney, *Our Inner Conflicts*, (New York: Norton, 1945), 96-114.

218 Rohr, *Immortal Diamond*, 28.

219 Henri Nouwen, *Home Tonight*, (New York: Doubleday, 2009), 108.

220 Etty Hillesum, *Etty Hillesum: An Interrupted Life the Diaries, 1941-1943 and Letters from Westerbork* (Picador, 1996). https://www.quotenik.com/etty-hillesum/

221 Frederick Buechner, *Now and Then*, (San Francisco, CA: HarperSanFrancisco, 1983), 87.

222 Richard Rohr, *Eager to Love*, (Cincinnati, Ohio: Franciscan Media, 2014), xiii.

223 G. Campbell Morgan, *The Westminster Pulpit*, Vol. 4, (Grand Rapids, MI: Baker Books, 1995), 206.

224 Klein, 3-4.

225 Klein, 27.

226 Os Guinness, *God in the Dark*, (Wheaton, Illinois: Crossway Books, 1996), 63.

227 Gary Klein, *Seeing What Others Don't: The Remarkable Ways We Gain Insights*, (New York: Public Affairs, 2013), 27.

228 Guinness, 62.

229 Matthew 14:22-33, Mark 6:45-52, John 6:16-21

230 David Jackman, *Mastering the Old Testament*, Volume 7: Judges, Ruth, (Dallas, TX: Word Publishing, 1991), 108.

231 Guinness, 71.

232 Brown, *Daring Greatly*, 121.

233 Greenspan, 156.

234 2 Corinthians 1:4, Isaiah 61:3

235 Albert Camus, *The Outsider*, (Penguin Classic, 2022). https://wordsfortheyear.com/tag/albert-camus/

236 Brené Brown, *Rising Strong*, (New York: Random House, 2017), xxv.

237 Western Folklore, Vol. 7, (California Folklore Society, 1948)

238 Freeman and DeWolf, 141.

239 Brené Brown, *Rising Strong*, (Random House, 2015). https://www.goodreads.com/work/quotes/42872911-rising-strong

240 F. W. Boreham, *The Golden Milestone* (London: Charles H Kelly, 1915), 57-58.

241 *Alcoholics Anonymous Big Book*. 4th ed. (New York, NY: Alcoholics Anonymous World Services., 2002)

242 Henri Nouwen, edited by Robert A. Jonas, *The Essential Henri Nouwen*, (Boston: Shambhala, 2009), 131-132.

243 "Trusting a Deeper Aliveness," Center for Action and Contemplation, September 4, 2020. https://cac.org/trusting-a-deeper-aliveness-2020-09-04/

244 Angela Duckworth, *Grit: The Power of Passion and Perseverance*, (New York: Scribner, 2016)

245 Duckworth, *Grit*, 150.

246 Richard Yates, *Revolutionary Road*, (New York: Vintage Books, 2000), 77-80.

247 William Damon, *The Path to Purpose*, (Free Press, 2009). https://parentotheca.com/2021/02/24/the-path-to-purpose-william-damon-book-summary/

248 Damon, *The Path to Purpose*

249 Lieberman and Long, 220.

250 Groopman

251 Lieberman and Long, 220.

252 Charles Reynolds Brown, "Charles Reynolds Brown papers, 1860-1957," https://hdl.handle.net/10079/bibid/747919

253 Groopman, 211.

254 "Hope" sermonsplus.co.ulk. http://www.sermonsplus.co.uk/Illustrations.htm

255 Dawson Church, *Mind to Matter*, (New York: Hay House, 2018), xi.

256 Leaf, 108.

257 Anders Ericsson and Robert Pool, *Peak: Secrets from the New Science of Expertise*, (Boston: Eamon Dolan Book, 2016), 19.

258 Ericsson and Pool, 19.

259 Ericsson and Pool, 38.

260 Ericsson and Pool, 39.

261 Ericsson and Pool, 41.

262 Klein, 84.

263 May, 121.

264 May, 85.

265 Margot Hornblower/Needles, "Heartbreak Motel" Time, May 29, 1995. http://content.time.com/time/subscriber/article/0,33009,982364,00.html

266 Brown, *Daring Greatly*, 116.

267 Rohr, *The Naked Now*, 90.

268 Leaf, 33.

269 Richard Rohr, *Breathing Under Water*, (Cincinnati, OH: Franciscan Media, 2011), 27.

270 Leaf, 33.

271 Rohr, *The Naked Now*, 90.

272 Richard Rohr, *Breathing Under Water*, (Cincinnati, OH: Franciscan Media, 2011), 27.

273 John Ortberg, *If You Want to Walk on Water, You've Got to Get Out of the Boat*, (Grand Rapids, MI: Zondervan, 2001), 95-96.

274 Ericsson and Pool, 169.

275 Ericsson and Pool, 169.

276 Ericsson and Pool, 169.

277 Shane J. Lopez, *Making Hope Happen*, (New York: Atria Books, 2013), 71.

278 Gabriele Oettingen, *Rethinking Positive Thinking*, (New York: Portfolio, 2015), xiv-xv.

279 Oettingen, xiv-xv.

280 Oettingen, xiv-xv.

281 Unknown. "The Boll Weevil Monument, Enterprise, Alabama.." Special Collections, USDA National Agricultural Library. Accessed March 8, 2024, https://www.nal.usda.gov/exhibits/speccoll/items/show/1060.

CONTINUE YOUR JOURNEY

AS YOU CONTINUE IN PURSUIT OF THE PERSON GOD CREATED
YOU TO BE, MAY YOU FIND THESE RESOURCES HELPFUL, AS WELL.

JOURNEY TO FREEDOM is a 36-day contemplative journey to help you understand your personal story and inner life more fully and compassionately. It will guide you through the stages needed for internal transformation, and allow you to find your own path toward emotional, spiritual and physical well-being.

JOURNEY TO WHOLENESS takes the reader on a 42-day contemplative journey filled with compassion, introspection, meaningful connection, and true hope while navigating a breast cancer diagnosis. This book will guide you through grieving what you have lost and help you move into a place of wholeness. Collaboratively written, Journey to Wholeness is the passion project of fellow survivors who know the gift of TRUE community and connection in the process of healing.

JOURNEY TO LIVING WITH COURAGE helps you address daily and persistent fears that impair your fullness of life. Fear is an inevitable part of being human, and it is a healthy part of your full emotional life when it functions to help you prepare, use discernment and keep you safe. But what happens when occasional fear turns to underlying worry and anxiety, robbing you of joy and peace? This book encourages you to acknowledge, expose and explore those persistent fears and the life experiences that inform them so that you can find a sense of security, practice courage, and move forward with hope.

JOURNEY TO A NEW BEGINNING AFTER LOSS helps heal the unacknowledged losses and disappointments in your life. From birth, you experience deeply profound losses that shape your story and circumstances. Your life is impacted by grief through intangible losses like unrealized dreams, unmet expectations, loss of innocence, trust, belonging, and self-worth. Or through tangible losses like finances, health, work, relationships, community, or death. Have you allowed yourself to truly grieve these losses? Do you feel that current losses bring up painful reminders of previous losses? Does lingering regret or resentment hold you back from a full life?

JOURNEY TO A LIFE OF SIGNIFICANCE helps you heal from the wounding of low self-worth. You may believe the lie that you will never be good enough, and so you strive to earn the love you long for and need. This book encourages honest self-reflection and movement toward acknowledging the inherent goodness and uniqueness God has placed in you. Uncover and examine the deeply rooted internal messages that hold you back from believing you are worthy, beloved or acceptable. Build a platform of self-worth to stand on that will positively impact all areas of your life.

PODCAST: Join us each week on the podcast *Searching Inward*

WEBSITE: restoresmallgroups.org

YOUTUBE CHANNEL: *A Moment of Hope* – @AMomentofHope-nu5dx